A Most Useful Prayer for the Traveller

Agla Pentagrammaton ✠ On ✠ Athanatos ✠ Anasareon ✠ On ✠ Pentareon ✠ Janua ✠ Crux ✠ Agraton ✠ Grex ✠ Lux ✠ Telatustus ✠ Hominis ✠ Tomon ✠ Tetragrammaton ✠ Jesus ✠ Deus ✠ Lord over all ✠ Merciful ✠ Most High ✠ my Saviour, deliver thy servant N. by these thy Holy Names; I am not worthy to call on thee, but remember me, Lord, who is everywhere, in thy mercy, and deliver me from the wiles of mine enemies, mine enemies, visible and invisible, and by the power of the Holy Cross and all thy Saints. Jesus ✠ passed among them, and departed. Jesus Christ ✠ Son of the Living God, have mercy upon me.

The Wandering School of Secrets
Copyright © 2025 Simon Dyda
Cover & interior artwork © Gero Casper
All Rights Reserved.

ISBN 978-1-915933-80-5 (Hardcover)
ISBN 978-1-915933-81-2 (Softcover)

A CIP catalogue for this title is available from the British Library.
10 9 8 7 6 5 4 3 2 1

Except in the case of quotations embedded in critical articles or reviews, no part of this book may be reproduced or transmitted in any form or by any means, electronic or mechanical, including photocopying, recording, or by any information storage and retrieval system, without permission in writing from the publisher.

No part of this book may be used or reproduced in any manner for the purpose of training artificial intelligence technologies or systems.

Simon Dyda has asserted his moral right to be identified as the author of this work.

Published in 2025
Hadean Press
West Yorkshire
England
hadean.press

The Wandering School of Secrets

A PROSPECTUS

by
Simon Dyda

illustrated by
Gero Casper

Dedicated to the memory of

Jake Stratton-Kent
1956 – 2023

without whose encouragement this work
would not have been written.

Requiescat in Potentia

Contents

Acknowledgements ix

I. VIA MAGISTER EST 1

II. MAGIA VIAM APERIT 5

    The Devil's Bible 9

    Casanova's Choice 12

III. SILENTIUM CLAVIS EST 15

IV. SUPERSTITIO RELIGIONEM SUPERSTAT 17

    The Warlock and the Mouse 23

V. SPIRITUS SOCII SUNT 26

VI. NOX INFERNUM EST 35

    An Archaic Eschatology 39

    Manifestations of the Netherworld 43

    Dream 44

    Dreaming like Rhonabwy 45

VII. SEPTEM SUNT 47

    The Seven Patrons 50

    Planetary Hours on the Road 68

    Planetary Chords 69

    The Planetary Rosary 69

VIII. MUNDUS NOBIS LOQUITUR 71

    Divination 73

IX. LEGENDA DEOS EVIGILAT   75

  Primary Texts   77

  Secondary Texts   79

  Bibliomancy   81

X. REX INFERNIS MUNDUM REGIT   83

  Veles   84

  Pan   85

XI. FORUM, FERIA ET PASTURA   88

XII. CANTATRIX IN LINGUAE UMBRARUM CANTAT   92

  Magical Language   92

  Demonic Macaronic   96

  Rhyme, Whispers, and Song   99

XIII. VINDICTA VENEFICIO VINCIT   101

  Exorcism by Knife   103

Bibliography   106

Index   112

Acknowledgements

The author would like to thank the following people who, knowingly or unknowingly, have assisted or inspired him during the composition of this work:

Aaman Lamba, Alexander Cummins, Alison Chicosky, Andrew Philip Smith, B.J. Swain, Bo Gjermandsen, Bob Phillips, Brian Johnson, Brigid Burke, Cath Thompson, Charles Porterfield, Colin Scallan, Chris Carr, Daniel Harms, Danu Stratton-Kent, David Rankine, Denis Poisson, Elise Oursa, Erzebet Barthold, Gero Casper, Grev Lyhne, Jake Stratton-Kent, Jason Spadafore, Jeff Lombardi, Jesse Hathaway Diaz, Joseph H. Peterson, Kadmus, Malte Mann, Mat Hadfield, Misha Newitt, Richard Voss, Rob Gygax, Sally North, Stephen Skinner, Steve Savedow, Stuart Innman and Sue Terry.

VIA MAGISTER EST

I

VIA MAGISTER EST

For as long as there has been travel, there have been travelling magicians and magic users. Travellers were always exposed to the dangers posed by climate, fauna, other humans, and malignant spirits, so they would employ magic in one form or another for protection and success in their endeavours.

For as long as there has been a legal distinction between licit and illicit magic there have been travelling practitioners of witchcraft, driven by the need to avoid entanglements with the authorities to wander from settlement to settlement and from city to city in order to ply their trade in charms, curses, love philtres, and divination. The legal distinction between licit and illicit forms of magic dates at least as far back as the *Code of Hammurabi* circa 1750 BCE.

Indeed, for much of its history, magic has been associated with itinerancy, and it is largely thanks to the itinerancy of sorcerers that the body of magical lore and techniques we now refer to as the Western Tradition was formed, disseminated, and perpetuated, both in Classical Antiquity and during the Middle Ages.

Magic has formed an integral part of consensus reality for most of human history, and although there exists today no lineage of magic in Europe that has been passed down from master to apprentice in an unbroken chain from antiquity to the present day, there has nevertheless very likely never been a time in the past four thousand years when there were no itinerant magicians; from the mendicant miracle workers and soothsayers of ancient Greece to the travelling magicians and astrologers of the Roman Empire; from the vagabond clerics of the Middle Ages to the wandering cunning folk of Early Modern England; from bohemian adventurers of the eighteenth century like Casanova and the Count of St Germain to the fairground fortune tellers of the modern era; and from the 'wickedest man in the world', Aleister Crowley, to 'Britain's most notorious necromancer', Jake Stratton-Kent.

Even in modern times, in which magic no longer forms part of consensus reality in the West, magic and its employment has endured among itinerants, not least because it is impossible to live 'on the road' without constantly witnessing and experiencing meaningful coincidences and epiphanies. It can be said with no exaggeration that the good fortunes of the wanderer frequently depend on a correct reading of such synchronicities and responding accordingly through the use of magic.

Liminal spaces are places of power in magic; they symbolise a gateway between this world and the Otherworld. It is in these spaces, be it a crossroads or a magic circle, that the magician's experience of the supernatural becomes intensified. The Road is itself a liminal space, and those who travel along it enter a liminal state of being throughout their journey between the place they have come from and the place they are

I. VIA MAGISTER EST

going. The same might be said of Life itself, but an actual journey magnifies the experience by giving the Cosmos and its spirits more opportunities to interact with the magician and more resources to attend to the magician's needs. It is perhaps for this reason that the magician is permitted a greater degree of flexibility to improvise while on the road than might otherwise be the case.

This experience is one that preserves the immanence of the divine or supernatural, which is made manifest in the mundane – an immanence the ancients were familiar with.

This need to employ magic for day-to-day life on the road is something we will refer to here as the Wandering School of Secrets. Although a purely figurative institution, it is in some regards superior to magical orders in which students often require years if not decades simply to break out of the scientific rationalist anti-magical mindset they were raised in, whereas the reality of magic and the supernatural quickly becomes apparent to students of the Wandering School; and while magical orders often require students to slowly progress through a series of grades before any actual magic gets done, the Wandering School instead requires its students to use magic straight away.

This book is intended to be a prospectus for those who wish to attend the Wandering School. Attending the Wandering School should furnish its students with the experience necessary to become proficient in sorcery. The road or journey itself will be their teacher – *via magister est*.

MAGIA VIAM APPERIT

II

MAGIA VIAM APERIT

A common misconception in modern occultism is that magic will only start working once the magician has overcome certain hurdles, such as learning to banish thought through meditation; correct breathing techniques; the building up or channelling of esoteric energies; physical and mental exhaustion; the use of narcotics; the study of psychology and/or neurology; the fortification of one's will power; or by developing one's 'psychic' abilities. Other supposed requisites include entering a trance state, or having an orgasm and then banishing any thoughts concerning the desired goal.

None of these things are necessary in magic. These hurdles have been imposed on magic by the mindset of late nineteenth and early twentieth century hipsters, a mindset which despite its spiritual and mystic pretensions was so anchored in rationalism that it could not believe that magic would work without a struggle. This mindset believed magic to be largely psychological in nature, that struggle had to be one concerned with consciousness and state of mind. The trendsetters of the so-called Occult Revival, rather than seeking out actual practitioners of Western magic, instead looked to Indian mysticism for inspiration, blending it with Western mysticism to create the fridge-raid soup of New

Age flakery, neopagan pantomime, and pseudomasonic pomposity that was characteristic of twentieth century esotericism and occultism.

According to this mindset, for magic to be real it must be especially difficult; requiring a trained singlemindedness and focus and/or some means of bypassing the mind in order to transcend the laws of physics and 'nudge probability' in a desired direction. If at any point this becomes easy, it should immediately be made more difficult in order to succeed.

All such statements as these are self-defeating nonsense: no special powers of focus, concentration, and attention beyond those required to perform any other task are necessary, and to engage in any power struggle with one's own mind is counterproductive and serves only to undermine the efficacy of the practitioner.

It should be pointed out at this juncture that the preceding paragraphs contain sweeping generalisations expressed in a deliberately irreverent manner regarding modern occultism. The Wandering School, as a purely figurative institution, does not dictate which system or tradition of magic its attendees should practice. However, its alumni will confirm the truth of the dictum *via magister est* and that the Road teaches us to discard any entrenched modern views we may have concerning magic and how magic is done. An inflexible adherence to such entrenched views will not put food in the magician's belly.

In traditional practices, magic is worked through an interaction between the magician and spirits, not through a struggle between the practitioner and their own mind. The magician need not hack their way through mental

II. MAGIA VIAM APERIT

undergrowth in order to perform magic; instead, magic itself opens the way to magic *magia viam aperit*. The only mental tool the magician requires is the imagination.

The key word in this use of the imagination is immersion. Anyone who has immersed themselves in a novel or a poem has experienced this magical state of consciousness in which perception is altered and extended by the imagination.

Immersion is facilitated by story. When performing magic, the magician will be calling upon story of one sort or another, be it in the form of verses from Holy Scripture, the deeds of deities in mythology, or the use of their epithets. For this reason it is important to familiarise ourselves with the myths, legends, or scripture relevant to the spirits we are engaging with.

We will talk more of the use of myth and story in magic anon. Of equal importance to the use of the imagination, the magician should avoid the pitfall of rationalisation when performing magic.

Many books on magic contain theories of magic which often amount to magician apologetics for either a medieval religious or a modern rationalist audience and are of no practical use beyond reassuring readers that the practice of magic is a sane and acceptable pursuit.

We learn from experience that magic works, but we cannot demonstrate why it works any more than a physicist can demonstrate why the laws of physics work the way they do.

It is far more productive to accept magic on its own terms, regardless of how 'unscientific' those terms might appear to be. The magician is not required to believe in magic for it to work; instead, the magician should disregard the question of belief entirely.

When we try to define magic using rationalist terms and try to make it fit into a rationalist paradigm, we undermine our ability to perform magic. Initially it may seem impossible to overcome our modern scepticism, to disregard our rationalist beliefs, but this difficulty is overcome by approaching magic with the attitude of a child at play. We have all been children, we have all played as children, and as adults we still immerse ourselves in our imaginations when we read a novel or when we daydream, so recovering a childlike attitude is not as hard a task as it might seem; it is, after all, literally child's play. If necessary, students can practice using games, gamebooks, and toys they liked as children, or by finding a group of tabletop RPG players they can play with before setting off on their journey with the Wandering School.

Real magical results are not necessarily accompanied by special effects. That is not to say that a magician will not see supernatural things when contacting or being contacted by certain spirits, but when it comes to the desired result we tasked the spirit to assist us with, the result will generally manifest itself in the form of a mundane coincidence. Even in the case of meeting the spirits, many will manifest themselves indirectly through mundane coincidences. We shall address the subjects of coincidences and spirits and their manifestation anon, but students should know right from the get go that they will not get a result or have an experience that scepticism cannot explain away.

Many veteran magicians will claim that one of their first successful magical operations produced a result that completely convinced them of the reality of magic. However, in many cases these veteran magicians are looking at their past experiences through rose-tinted glasses, and have been magicians for so long that they have simply forgotten that the reality of magic ever came into question.

For sedentary magicians, it can take years to be truly convinced of the reality of magic, because of the level of their engagement with the scientistic rationalist model of reality and because their magical successes can be explained away.

In contrast, the student of the Wandering School will experience the reality of magic with such frequency and regularity that all doubts and explanations that scepticism might present us with become entirely irrelevant.

THE DEVIL'S BIBLE

The student should be in possession of a grimoire, spellbook, or book of shadows. Such books were sometimes referred to as 'devil's Bibles', an apt enough description for reasons that will have become clear by the end of this prospectus.

Working with a grimoire often involves planning, preparation, and timing, and as such needs to be supplemented by spells and charms that students can deploy for their immediate needs on the road. These spells and charms generally belong to the category of folk magic, although even folk magic requires some preparation, and so students will have to learn how to improvise, supported by their spirit allies.

The modern student has access to an important piece of technology that no previous generation of students had, namely the e-reader, which allows individuals to have their own portable libraries. However, such devices need constant recharging, can be adversely affected by the use of magic, and often prove too fragile for life on the road. For this reason the student should possess a physical book and not be exclusively dependent on e-readers. Students are also strongly discouraged from engaging in online activities and social media while attending the Wandering School and should instead be fully engaged with their surroundings. Furthermore, physical books have a talismanic value that electronic books do not possess.

For absolute newcomers to magic, we recommend *Mastering Witchcraft* and also *Mastering Herbalism* by Paul Huson (the latter can be followed with Catherine Yronwode's *Hoodoo Herb and Root Magic*). For newcomers to astrological magic, also known as astral magic, we recommend *Mansions of the Moon* and also *Secrets of Planetary Ritual* by Christopher Warnock. Other works on magic recommended for beginners are *Six Ways* by Aidan Wachter; *Communing with the Spirits* by John M Hansen; *Consorting with Spirits* by Jason Miller; and both *Night School Volume I: The Sworn & Secret Grimoire* and *Night School Volume II: Cyprian's Offices of Spirits* by Jake Stratton-Kent. *Claves Intelligentiarum* by David Rankine offers a step-by-step guide to the conjuration of spirits, and

II. MAGIA VIAM APERIT

Professor Charles Porterfield's *A Deck of Spells* is essential reading for cartomancy.

Finding the right grimoire is part of the learning process; we recommend that students consult David Rankine's *Grimoire Encyclopaedia* volume 1 on this matter. The chosen book may become a lifelong companion, or merely the first of many; or the sorcerer may ultimately find that a mere handful of spells and materials suffices for all their needs. A master aims at economy of operations, not proliferation, and so the magician's work might eventually centre around the use of a single object, a 'special piece', which might be a wand, a pipe, a knife, a set of beads, or a deck of cards.

As mentioned in the previous chapter, the liminal nature of the Wandering School affords its students a greater degree of flexibility to improvise: a chalice, athame, and magic wand, for example, might be substituted in a pinch by a paper cup, a plastic knife, and a twig. For ideas and inspiration in this area we recommend students familiarise themselves with some of the techniques used in Hoodoo, the African American tradition of folk magic which is the fruit of improvisation and adaptation on the part of its practitioners, becoming perhaps the finest tradition of folk magic in the western world and one that has a wealth of techniques suited to life on the road. A good place to begin is with *The Hoodoo Bible* by Mama Marie, and Professor Charles Porterfield's *The Sporting Life* is of particular relevance to the milieu of the itinerant sorcerer.

Another American tradition of folk magic, Pow Wow, the folk magic of the Pennsylvania Dutch, can be found in America's oldest grimoire, *The Long-Lost Friend*. Other folk magic grimoires suitable for use on the road are *The Sixth and Seventh Book of Moses* (edited by Joseph Peterson), *The Book of Gold* (edited by David Rankine), *The Grimoire of Arthur Gauntlet* (edited by David Rankine) and *Enchiridion Leonis Papae* (translated by Paul Summers-Young).

CASANOVA'S CHOICE

In 1755 the adventurer Giacomo Casanova (1725-1798) owned five bound manuscripts on magic, confiscated by the State Inquisition of Venice in July of that year. The five books included:

The Key of Solomon the King
The Zecorben
The Picatrix
A book of Instructions on the Planetary Hours
The necessary incantations for conversing with demons of all sorts

Casanova wrote: 'Those who were aware that I possessed these books took me for an expert magician, and I was not sorry to have such a reputation.'[1]

This selection can be emulated with the following books:

---

[1] Giacomo Casanova, *The Memoirs of Jacques Casanova de Seingalt*, Vol. II, trans. by Arthur Machen (Arthur Machen, 1894).

II. MAGIA VIAM APERIT

1. *The Veritable Key of Solomon* by Stephen Skinner and David Rankine; or *The Clavis or Key of the Magic of Solomon* by Joseph H. Peterson.
2. *True Black Magic* by Joseph H. Peterson.
3. *The Complete Picatrix* by John Michael Greer and Christopher Warnock.
4. *The Book of the Moon – Liber Lunae* by Don Karr and Stephen Skinner.
5. *Elucidation of Necromancy* by Joseph H. Peterson.

SILENTIUM CLAVIS EST

III

SILENTIUM CLAVIS EST

Secrecy is important in sorcery for a number of reasons.

Disclosing to others what magical operation or magical experiment you are about to do, or are currently engaged in, or have recently done, invites interference on all levels of reality. In addition to this concern, it trivialises the operation, stripping it of its proper dignity, treating the supernatural as mundane and the sacred as profane, thereby causing the spirits involved if not the cosmos as a whole to cease to take the sorcerer seriously. A lack of secrecy is the surest way for an operation to fail. *Silentium clavis est*, silence is the key.

As well as such practical and spiritual reasons, there are also precautionary and strategic reasons for secrecy. For instance, you will have random encounters with indiscrete individuals who will almost immediately inform you that they are sorcerers or witches or some other type of practitioner, and they will often be narcissists and sociopaths who will treat any revelation on your part of a knowledge of sorcery as an infringement on their domain and a direct challenge. If they are ignorant of the fact that you are a sorcerer, then should they attempt to use magic to harm you, they will be careless and easily foiled.

While on the road, it is generally impractical to call attention to your interest in sorcery. As an itinerant you will most likely be seen as a vagabond Bohemian; adding any overt occultist leanings will only make life harder, placing unnecessary obstacles in your way.

Furthermore, although many of us live in countries where it might seem that we are free to publicly identify ourselves as sorcerers and witches, history informs us unambiguously that such freedom fluctuates. Even in countries where the practice of sorcery and witchcraft is currently legal, in most cases it is contrary to the accepted norms of the society we live in, and this was the case even when a belief in magic formed part of consensus reality.

For itinerants, this fluctuation of freedom is often evident within their own lifetimes. In Europe, the freedom to travel and the freedom to make a living as a street entertainer fluctuates from year to year and decade to decade and has done so since antiquity.

Irrespective of the student's spiritual tradition, the practice of magic is generally considered to be a subversive and unorthodox pursuit, and a lack of secrecy while attending the Wandering School will invite interference and place unnecessary obstacles in the student's path which may undermine the whole purpose of attending.

IV

SUPERSTITIO RELIGIONEM SUPERSTAT

The practice of magic has long been contrary to societal norms and the orthodoxy of religious authorities, even before the advent of Christianity. As mentioned in Chapter I, a legal distinction between licit and illicit forms of magic dates at least as far back as the *Code of Hammurabi*.

The *Code of Hammurabi* is a Babylonian legal text composed c. 1755 -1750 BCE. It contains two hundred and eighty-two laws, and the second of these laws states that 'If a man charge a man with sorcery, and cannot prove it, he who is charged with sorcery shall go to the river, into the river he shall throw himself and if the river overcome him, his accuser shall take to himself his house (estate). If the river shows that man to be innocent and he comes forth unharmed, he who charged him with sorcery shall be put to death. He who threw himself into the river shall take to himself the house of his accuser.'[2]

The translators of the *Code of Hammurabi* and other Mesopotamian tablets employ the English terms 'sorcery' and 'witchcraft' to describe illicit forms of magic, and the terms 'sorcerer', 'witch', and 'warlock' to describe

---

2 W.W. Davies, *The Codes of Hammurabi and Moses* (Cornell University Library 2009), pp. 23-24.

any practitioner of illicit magic. The Mesopotamian term for witchcraft was *uš*, meaning 'spittle'.[3]

There were licit forms of magic sanctioned by the civic and religious authorities in Mesopotamia, but these were practiced by priests trained to be professional exorcists known as the *ašipu*, meaning 'user of incantations'. As malevolent spirits, of their own accord, or witchcraft involving the use of ghosts and demons, was thought to be the cause of illness and disease, the exorcist was employed to combat these curses by exorcising the malignant spirits involved. In addition to this role as healer, the exorcist would be called upon in the consecration of temples, ensuring that the temple was free of any evil spirits; similarly he would be called upon in the appointment of new priests to ensure that they were spiritually clean. The exorcist relied on omens in his diagnosis of illness and his judgements regarding the spiritual cleanliness of people and places, and was expert in the rites and incantations that would provide favourable and fortunate outcomes where otherwise ill-fortune was a certainty. The magic of the exorcist invoked the divine power of the gods, but sometimes employed demons against other demons, such as in the case of Pazuzu, who could protect pregnant women from the infanticidal demoness Lamashtu.

In contrast, the sorcerer could offer his clients those services the exorcist could not or would not offer, catering to their unholy desires: love, sex, fame and

---

[3] Interestingly, spittle plays an important role in the lore of Egyptian magic. See *The Mechanics of Ancient Egyptian Magical Practice* by Robert K. Ritner.

fortune and of course misfortune, distress, and harm to rivals and enemies.

Over a thousand years later in Ancient Greece, the situation for the sorcerer was hardly any better. Magicians could find themselves charged with impiety, and if found guilty, sentenced to death. A sorcerer could be beaten up and driven out of the city, either as an individual or as part of a purge of undesirables. Sporadic mass expulsions and mass executions of magicians and astrologers would later become a feature of Roman rule. Magic has therefore become a fundamentally subversive pursuit, and even when it forms part of the same spiritual tradition to which the rest of society belongs, it is fundamentally heterodox.

This subversive heterodoxy is evident among many of the sorcerers of Late Antiquity, such as those who used the spells of the so-called Greek Magical Papyri. For these sorcerers, all spirits and deities were potential allies, regardless of which culture or religion they belonged to.

The Wandering School of Secrets, being a purely figurative institution, is open to students from any spiritual tradition and to practitioners of any system of magic, but within the confines of this prospectus it is a school of witchcraft and sorcery which subscribes to the mindset of the aforementioned sorcerers of Late Antiquity and engages with Abrahamic spirits as well as pagan ones. In the case of pagan and diabolist spirits, we have the option of subversively employing syncretism to disguise these relationships; in the case of Christian or Jewish spirits where disguise is not necessary, pagan students can familiarise themselves with the pagan origins of these spirits, how they may be employed in a pagan context, and should be aware that for the true pagan all spirits are pagan spirits.

A pagan happens to be passing a shrine of St Anthony when he discovers that he has lost his wallet. Should he then think: 'Well here's a stroke of luck, I happen to be in the presence of a specialist in recovering lost property' and then proceed to engage the assistance of the saint, he is demonstrating the mindset of both a true sorcerer and a true pagan. If instead he shuns the very thought of approaching a Christian saint for help, he is demonstrating the mindset of a Christian fundamentalist and a D&D cleric.

Magic is not a religion, and in truth, magic or sorcery is not so much a heterodoxy as it is a heteropraxy. The Latin term *religio* from which the word 'religion' derives originally referred to the Roman Cult of the Gods or *Cultus Deorum*, which, like modern-day Shinto in Japan, was an orthopraxy and not an orthodoxy. It had no doctrines, no dogma, no official theology, and no sacred texts. Instead it had rules regarding the correct performance of its rites and ceremonies. The correct performance of these rites ensured that the gods would be benevolent towards the Roman State and its people. Individuals could petition the gods for favours in exchange for offerings and a promise of further offerings to come, and would approach the gods as humble supplicants.

Practices that did not conform with these norms – including sorcery – were categorised as *superstitio*, a

IV. SUPERSTITIO RELIGIONEM SUPERSTAT

term from which the word 'superstition' is derived. *Superstitio* came to mean more or less the same thing as 'superstition', but originally it came from the verb *superstare*, meaning both 'to stand over, above' and also 'to survive' and thus perhaps first referred to indigenous Italian cults that had survived the Romanisation of Italy. By the time *superstitio* had acquired the same meaning as the English word 'superstition', Romans had to reinvent the connection to its source verb *superstare*, which they did by explaining that it described the condition of being excessively fearful of the gods who 'stood over them'; however, the suffix *-tio* simply provides the noun form of a verb and nothing more elaborate than that, thus *superstitio* denotes the act of standing above or the act of surviving. If we look elsewhere among Indo-European languages for exact literal equivalents of *superstare* (over+stand we find the German *überstehen*, meaning 'to survive; to rise above; to stand above'; and the Welsh *gorsefyll*, which the *University of Wales Dictionary* defines as 'to resist, withstand, oppose; stay, stand, stand still; loiter, linger; delay, stay; continue to exist, subsist, hold out; encamp, be stationed.'

At the same time, the term was applied to practices that were considered too gaudy for Roman sensibilities, so we might interpret *superstare* as meaning 'to stand out', that is to say, to be something that is 'over the top'. Christianity was classed as *superstitio*, and certainly Christians were considered 'over the top' in their refusal to participate in those public observations that the Roman State believed to be essential for maintaining good relations with the gods.

There is another possible meaning we might give to the verb *superstare*, one that is relevant to the practice of sorcery, which is that the sorcerer does not approach the gods as a supplicant, but as an equal partner and sometimes even threatens or bullies them. Indeed, the collection of spells known as the Greek Magical Papyri indicate that the sorcerer might play all three roles – supplicant, equal, and bully – within the same spell. Thus we might choose to interpret *superstare* to mean 'to stand above' religious supplication and its passive acceptance of the will of the gods and fate, a blasphemous act which would inevitably lead to the religiously devout defining *superstare* as meaning 'to act above one's station', 'get above oneself', or 'get uppity'.

This 'uppity' attitude towards the gods was precisely the reason why Plato and Platonists were so antagonistic towards magicians, condemning them to death for their apparent impiety.

The Wandering School encourages both heterodoxy and heteropraxy and in that spirit proclaims *superstitio religionem superstat*, which can be taken to mean 'superstition (sorcery) stands above religion' and 'superstition survives religion'. The sorcerer also stands above religious and spiritual dichotomies such as paganism vs Christianity, polytheism vs monotheism, spiritual vs material, Heaven vs Hell, right hand vs left hand, beneficium vs maleficium, piety vs impiety, and even *superstitio* vs *religio*.

IV. SUPERSTITIO RELIGIONEM SUPERSTAT

THE WARLOCK AND THE MOUSE

To the best of our knowledge, the word 'warlock' has no exact equivalent in non-Germanic languages. It does not simply mean 'a male witch' or 'sorcerer' – there's more to its meaning than that.

The etymology of 'warlock' is as follows: the word derives from the Middle English *warloghe*, *warlowe*, *warloȝe*, from Old English *wǣrloga* ('traitor, deceiver' literally 'truce-breaker'), from *wǣr* ('covenant, truce, pact, promise'), from Proto-Indo-European **wēr-* ('true'); and from *loga* ('liar'), from Proto-Germanic **lugô*, related to Old English *lēogan* ('lie'). The hard -ck ending originated in Scots and Northern English, and it is actually the Scottish form 'warlock' ('male magic-user', from the notion that such men were in league with the Devil) that is now used in English. It is cognate with Old High German *wārlogo* ('truce-breaker, traitor').

So why exactly is a warlock a 'truce breaker'? The answer, we would suggest, can be found in the collection of essays titled *Gair am Air* by the Welsh scholar Gwyn Thomas.

The 'truce' is Tradition, that is to say, the 'truce' between mankind and the spirits (or gods).

'Ancestors and tradition – the way things were done by custom – had an important place in the beliefs of the Celts and their way of life (the same was true for other peoples too). One scholar, Maartje Draak, went as far as to say: *It is impossible [for the Celts] to explain any catastrophe as the Will of God, or Whim of God; it must be the result of some untraditional act by a human being.*'[4] He adds: 'You cannot pray, you cannot ask for forgiveness; in the end, there is only one way to solve things – magic.'[5]

By breaking this 'truce' – deliberately going against tradition and custom by breaking a taboo – the sorcerer engages the Otherworld and its denizens.

Manawydan has grown fields of corn, but a plague of mice are destroying the corn. He watches and catches one of them. He decides to hang the mouse as a thief. Hang a mouse! Cigfa, who's a bit of a snob, does not approve of such a thing – a man of Manawydan's honour going to do something so uncustomary as hanging a mouse. You see that the point is made quite clear: by hanging a mouse Manawydan would be committing an act that is contrary to custom – an act not too dissimilar from that of Pwyll driving away the hounds of Arawn from the stag.

But Manawydan knows what he is doing: he is challenging Annwn. He is placing himself in the between state. The powers of Annwn take the bait. As Manawydan builds a gallows for the mouse on Gorsedd Arberth, who comes by but a cleric. At this point, Manawydan has not seen a living soul for seven years! Who greets whom first? The cleric. Manawydan has the advantage. The cleric, like Cigfa, tries to persuade him

---

4 Original footnote: Maartje Draak, 'The Religion of the Celts', in C. Jouco Bleaker and Geo Widengren, *Historia Religionum*, 1 (Leiden, 1969), pp. 3, 640.

5 Original translation from the Welsh by Simon Dyda from *Gair am Air* by Gwyn Thomas (University of Wales Press 2000), excerpted from pages 27-31.

IV. SUPERSTITIO RELIGIONEM SUPERSTAT

not to perform such a base act. He offers a payment to Manawydan not to perform an act so beneath his status, but Manawydan refuses. The same happens with a passing priest. Then, a bishop and his retinue pass by. This time Manawydan is the first to greet, but note what he says: 'Lord bishop...thy blessing'. The bishop must give his blessing, and by doing so places Manawydan in an affirmative position. If anyone wants a lesson on how to draw up a contract they should study the part of the story that follows, where Manawydan puts the powers of Annwn in such a corner that they cannot move without losing everything.

Then, it is explained to us that a woman in the form of a mouse is the one that Manawydan wishes to hang: the wife of Llwyd fab Cil Coed, the one who is in the form of a bishop.

Religio is about establishing and maintaining a pact with the gods, of which we will discuss in the next chapter; the sorcerer both makes and breaks this pact as the situation may require. This is the fundamental difference between religion and sorcery: the former submits unconditional obedience to the gods while the latter only offers them conditional obedience.

V

SPIRITUS SOCII SUNT

Sorcery is defined in the *Miriam Webster Dictionary* as being 'the use of power gained by the assistance or control of evil spirits', the 'evil' spirits in question being any spirit the Church disapproves of, which is most spirits. A less biased definition of sorcery might be to describe it as being magic that employs spirits to achieve desired goals. *Spiritus socii sunt* – spirits are our allies. So what are spirits?

Everything possesses being: a fish possesses fish being, a chair possesses chair being, the wind possesses wind being, and even the symbolism of an image and the movement of a planet as seen from Earth possess their own forms of being. Myths, stories, and words have being, as do mythological and fictional characters.

There are those who believe that the verb *to be* implies a static state that is not representative of the dynamic nature of reality. There is no *is*, they suggest; only does. Ironically perhaps, this is a thoroughly materialist interpretation of language; *to be* is a verb and verbs describe action. To say 'a spade is a spade' is in fact to say 'a spade is being a spade.' Thus the statement 'a spade is a spade' only appears to infer a static state when looked at through a materialist lens.

The statement 'a spade is being a spade' is, on an atomic level, literally and objectively true, yet also

V. SPIRITUS SOCII SUNT

implies that the spade possesses some form of agency and identity or personhood of its own; in other words, that the spade is a being. Once we begin to entertain the notion that the spade is a being, we part ways with the materialist model of reality and enter an animist paradigm.

As infants and young children we inevitably humanise many of the non-human things we encounter, both animate and inanimate, and are further encouraged to do so by our culture, in which children are entertained with tales of talking fauna and flora, talking vehicles, toys that come to life when nobody is looking as well as more traditional fairytales and legends rooted in an animist worldview. By way of both nature and nurture then, an animist model of reality is the first one we are introduced to. Even as adults we may find ourselves reverting to animism when an inanimate object becomes a source of irritation, a situation hilariously portrayed in the scene from the comedy Fawlty Towers in which the character Basil Fawlty gives his stalled car 'a damn good thrashing' to punish it for its apparent intransigence.

The sorcerer lives in an animist universe; a universe in which all things, both visible and invisible, both corporeal and incorporeal, possess being. Among these forms of being, particularly among those categorised as invisible and incorporeal, are the various supernatural entities collectively classed as spirits.

It is perhaps useful here to look to a living animist tradition for an answer that is of practical use to the sorcerer, specifically Shinto and its cult of the *kami*, a Japanese term for certain gods, fairies, and spirits.

Firstly it should be noted that Shinto has no fixed set of beliefs or doctrines regarding the nature of the kami. In Shinto, what one does is important, not what one believes. Correct action and the use of correct etiquette when venerating the kami is all-important, not what one might believe the kami to be.

We find a parallel to this emphasis on correct etiquette among the pagan priests of ancient Rome, where a single mistake in the performance of a public ceremony would result in the entire ceremony having to be redone, even when the mistake occurred at the end of a three-day-long ceremony. For the Romans this was important to ensure the 'Peace of the Gods' or *Pax Deorum*, and here we find another parallel with Shinto: irrespective of the different views regarding the nature of the kami, everyone involved agrees that the veneration of the kami is necessary to ensure peaceful relations with them and the prosperity and well-being of society.

It was this requirement to ensure the *Pax Deorum* that became the major bone of contention between early Christians and the authorities of pagan Rome. As pagan polytheists, the Romans rarely questioned the validity and existence of foreign deities, and therefore could not comprehend why a foreign cult might question the validity of Roman gods. Everyone was expected to participate in the public celebrations of the gods of Rome, regardless of what their spiritual tradition might be, in order to ensure the *Pax Deorum*; and it was a source of frustration and vexation for the Romans that Christians refused to do this.

V. SPIRITUS SOCII SUNT

Returning our attention to the kami, to begin with we can sort them into five categories. The first category are the kami of myth and legend, particularly those myths related to the creation of the world and of Japan. These are in many regards equivalent to the gods and titans of European and Mediterranean mythologies, and as is the case in Western myth-cycles, many of the first gods or titans to come into existence have no cults of their own and have no function beyond describing how the world came into being and is the way it is. In this category we find the greatest of all the kami: the sun goddess Amaterasu.

The second category is that of nature spirits, the spirits of particular locations in nature such as a mountain, a forest, a tree, a glade, a grove, a river, or a spring. We find their equivalent in the elves, trolls, dryads, nymphs, numens, and fairies of Europe.

The third category is that of the ancestors. The ancestors as kami watch over their family or clan and protect their descendants. In some cases an ancestral kami might also belong to one of the other categories listed here, the prime example being the sun goddess Amaterasu who is the ancestress of the emperors of Japan. In the West there are many instances of divine or supernatural ancestry: the pharaohs of Egypt were the children of Amun-Ra; Helios is the ancestor of witches; the Juliae of Rome were descendants of Venus; the Gauls were descended from Dis Pater: medieval Welsh genealogies all lead back to mythological figures; and people descended from fairies and other supernatural entities are found in folklore everywhere.

The fourth category of kami are the souls of great people. People who were renowned masters in an occupation or field of interest have become the patron kami of those professions and fields of interest. The Western equivalent might be saints and heroes. It should be noted here that, regardless of the association between such a kami and the thing they were masters of in life, any kami can grant any prayer. That is to say, although a practitioner might travel to the shrine of the kami of hair in order to pray for a cure for baldness, technically that practitioner's local kami can be petitioned to grant that wish. We find something similar in the West where a demon, saint, angel or elf might assist a magician even in matters they are not primarily associated with.

The fifth category is that of the Emperors, both the current Emperor and his deceased ancestors. We might draw parallels with the divinity of pharaohs, deified Roman emperors and the divine right to rule of medieval kings.

Not all kami are benevolent; some kami are malevolent, dreadful, dangerous, or uncanny, in which case they are venerated in order to placate them and thereby deter them from causing harm. The kami of volcanoes are an example of dangerous spirits whose veneration is primarily intended to placate them and thereby avoid a catastrophe. Chopped animal parts left by Icelanders in the Surtshellir lava cave may have been offerings intended to serve the same purpose, and other examples of dangerous spirits that need to be placated can be found in traditions all around the world.

V. SPIRITUS SOCII SUNT

Not all spirits are kami: ghosts and other 'unclean' spirits are not venerated but instead are exorcised by Shinto priests. There are other supernatural entities in Japanese folklore with whom a sorcerer might interact that are not classed as kami, such as the *yokai*.

In practice, the kami are invisible beings who can hear and grant wishes in exchange for respect, veneration, and offerings. Some kami have visual representations, some do not. Images of kami are thought to be able to house those kami, and the representations of kami on altars at home – purchased from the priests at their shrines – are believed to contain part of the kami. Again we find parallels of this belief in Western traditions, Christian as well as pagan.

Thus far we have only touched upon 'traditional' conceptions of the kami, or rather 'practical' conceptions of them. As invisible spirits we can, using the verb 'to be' as our criteria, affirm that they have being, but so do visible things like our aforementioned spade. We have already established that our spade is a being, but it is definitely not an invisible spirit that can hear and grant wishes, therefore *spirit* and *being* are distinct categories. This distinction, however, becomes blurred when we consider the beliefs of Shinto practitioners concerning the nature of the kami.

One widely-accepted definition is that a kami can be anything that has an outstanding impact on people's lives, be it a mythological or fictional character, a spectacular natural phenomenon, or an exceptional human being. In this context the term 'kami' refers to a quality, a quality we might render in English as 'divine' or 'holy'. Using this as our yardstick, anything that has being can be a kami so long as it is in some way exceptional.

A mountain might be thought by some to be the home of a kami, while others believe that the mountain itself is the kami. In other words, some view the kami as being the spirit of a thing, while others view the kami as the being of a thing. Both views agree that the thing itself is in some way exceptional or remarkable.

A similar overlap between spirit and being exists in Western traditions, but in the practice of sorcery and witchcraft the term 'spirit' is generally used in three different contexts.

In the first, supernatural entities and the spirits of the dead are referred to collectively as 'spirits'.

In the second place, anything in the natural world possesses both being and spirit. In this context, 'spirit' is often synonymous with 'life force'. Indeed, the word is derived from the word for 'breath', as are the words for 'spirit' and 'soul' in many languages.

In the third place we have artificial things, both physical and conceptual, which can be imbued with spirit by the sorcerer or, put another way, which have a dormant spirit that the sorcerer can awaken.

All that said, the difference between spirit and being is largely semantic. Turning to the animist traditions of indigenous Australian cultures, the term 'dreaming' is used in place of both spirit and being and goes a step further than these two words, as the word dreaming implies a form of sentience, In Aboriginal cultures, everything has a dreaming; in other words, everything

V. SPIRITUS SOCII SUNT

has spirit, being, and sentience. What is more, the dreaming of a thing is also the myth and lore of that thing: spirit and story are inseparable. We have already mentioned the importance of myth and story in magic and will return to this subject anon.

As we have seen above, despite any differences between Western and Japanese ideas of spirits and divinity, comparisons can be made between the various kinds of kami and the spirits of Western traditions, making Shinto perhaps easier for the Western neo-animist to comprehend than might be the case with other animist traditions around the world. In many of the aboriginal traditions of Australia, for example, most if not all of the non-human kami would qualify as being ancestral beings who at the same time are nature spirits and characters in myth.

As mentioned above, the sorcerer employs the assistance of spirits. In order to do so, sorcerers must first establish a relationship with the spirits they wish to employ. These relationships are reciprocal ones in that the sorcerer makes offerings to the spirits in exchange for their assistance.

Providing spirits with regular offerings is critical to establishing and maintaining a relationship with them. These offerings generally consist of lit candles or oil lamps, the burning of incense, a libation, food and an incantation, hymn, or prayer. For the itinerant sorcerer, the most convenient combination is that of an incantation, hymn, or prayer and a libation of water.

When offering incense, many spirits have a preference for specific incenses, and some incenses are unsuitable for certain spirits. Frankincense is generally acceptable to all spirits.

In preparation for their attendance of the Wandering School of Secrets, students should spend a season establishing and then strengthening some basic spirit relationships. First and foremost among these are ancestral spirits, which we shall discuss in the next chapter.

VI

NOX INFERNUM EST

The first spirits with whom sorcerers should establish a relationship are the spirits of their ancestors. Establishing a relationship with our ancestors ensures that they provide us with their protection and their assistance and grants us access to their experience and knowledge. In the case of ancestors who we don't like or who are at odds with us, this practice can be used to mollify them and neutralise any negative interference.

Most Westerners will have Christian ancestors who, before the Reformation, would have been members of either a Catholic or an Orthodox congregation. Prior to that they would have been pagans and animists, but our first Christian ancestors act as a bridge to our last pagan ancestors, just as our first *Homo sapiens* and Neanderthal ancestors act as a bridge to their more archaic predecessors. For this reason the Wandering School recommends to those of Christian heritage the employment of Christian practices when honouring our ancestors.

An additional benefit of using Christian practices to engage with our ancestors is that when we then use Christian forms of sorcery and folk magic, such as the use of psalms as incantations, their potency is enhanced by our connection to ancestral spirits.

VI. NOX INFERNUM EST

Students can also visit Catholic or Orthodox churches, chapels, and shrines where they can light candles and recite a psalm as an offering to their ancestors and to any saint whose assistance or patronage they seek, or to a deity they have syncretised with that saint.

A practice that has become increasingly popular among magicians in the twenty-first century is the setting up of an altar in their homes specific to the veneration of ancestors, but a student of the Wandering School can hardly take such an altar with them on the road. The student must devise their own practice and method for venerating ancestors, but one method we can recommend to students with Catholic ancestry is the recitation of the Holy Rosary using a set of rosary beads.

In addition to the Holy Rosary, there is also the Requiem for souls in Purgatory:

Requiem aeternam dona eis, Domine, et lux perpetua luceat eis, requiescant in pace. Amen.

May they be given eternal rest, O Lord, and may perpetual light shine upon them, may they rest in peace. Amen.

The word *Domine* (O Lord) can be switched to *Domina* (O Lady) if preferred; and the Hebrew *Amen* can be switched with the Latin *Esto*.

An alternative to the prayer for souls in Purgatory is the prayer for souls in Paradise:

Gaudium aeternum dona eis, Domina, et lux perpetua luceat eis, residant in paradiso. Esto.

May eternal joy be given them, O Lady, and may perpetual light shine upon them, may they reside in paradise. May it be so.

Another alternative to *Requiescant in pace* is *Requiescant in potentia*, 'May they rest in power'.

Those of Christian and Jewish heritage can recite a psalm, such as Psalm 130 (Vulgate Psalm 129), known in Latin as *De Profundis* ('from the depths'). Whatever your heritage might be, there will be prayers for the dead you can use. The key factor is to employ prayers that will be familiar to your most recent ancestors.

Another way of honouring ancestors is to adhere to an ancestral code of behaviour, or to a code of behaviour of the student's own creation devised to honour ancestors. These might reflect the religious heritage of the student, or might be sourced from mythology and folklore. One example of the latter is the advice given to Peredur by his mother as he sets out in search of adventure:

> 'Go forward, then,' she said, 'to the Court of Arthur, where there are the best, and the boldest, and the most bountiful of men. And wherever thou seest a church, recite there thy Paternoster unto it. And if thou seest meat and drink, and have need of them, and none have the kindness or the courtesy to give them

to thee, take them thyself. If thou hearest an outcry, proceed towards it, especially if it be the outcry of a woman. If thou seest a fair jewel, possess thyself of it, and give it to another, for thus thou shalt obtain praise. If thou seest a fair woman, pay thy court to her, whether she will or no; for thus thou wilt render thyself a better and more esteemed man than thou wast before.'[6]

The most appropriate time to make offerings to ancestors is at dusk or after nightfall, and here we come to another factor that is of importance when sorcerers venerate their ancestors, because this timing for veneration links us to our most archaic of human ancestors – not only early *Homo sapiens*, but also *Homo neanderthalensis*, *Homo heidelbergensis*, and other archaic humans.

AN ARCHAIC ESCHATOLOGY

Archaic humans walked the earth for over a million years and over a wide geographical area spanning the continents of Africa, Europe, and Asia and inhabited a variety of climates. Consequently the diet, technology, and culture of archaic humans varied according to time and location. The same is true of their mortuary practices, and doubtlessly was also true regarding any cosmological and eschatological beliefs they might

---

6 *Y Mabinogion*, ed. by Rhiannon and Dafydd Ifans, passage trans. by Simon Dyda (Gwasg Gomer, 2001), p. 170.

have had. Nevertheless, there is what we might call a primal cosmology that arguably could have occurred to archaic humans, one that could have been arrived at independently by members of every species of human, and one that was indeed arrived at by members of our own species.

This primal cosmology is based on the simplest and most basic of correspondences and therefore does not require the same level of cognitive intelligence as that of modern humans in order to be arrived at.

This primal cosmology is a two-fold division of the world into the Dayworld and the Nightworld, with the Dayworld being the realm of the Living; and the Nightworld being the realm of the Sleeping, Dreams, and the Dead. *Nox Infernum est*, 'the Night is the Netherworld'.

This cosmology is anchored in experiential reality: the Sleeping resemble the Dead and vice versa; and in dreams we can encounter dead acquaintances. We sleep and dream during the night; and the darkness is full of deadly perils. It is perhaps reflected in the placement of the dead in natural subterranean chambers, often difficult to access, the logic perhaps being that these dark places by virtue of their permanent sunlessness belonged to the Nightworld.

This primal cosmology develops into an archaic eschatology with the addition of a third component to the two worlds of the primal cosmology, namely the Red Gates of Dusk and Dawn.

This is perhaps indicated by the use of the colour red in connection with funerary practices. We have the

VI. NOX INFERNUM EST

use of red ochre in funerary rites among both *Homo neanderthalensis* and *Homo sapiens*.

Red ochre had many uses;: it was used as a pigment, as a sun-block, as an antifungal and antibacterial salve both for medicinal purposes and in the tanning of hides, as an ointment to protect the skin from insect bites, and as an adhesive, to name but a few of its uses. With the many uses of red ochre, the colour of sunrise and sunset and the colour of blood, we can be fairly certain that red was the colour of magic as far as archaic humans were concerned.

We also have the three hundred and fifty thousand year-old red quartz axe of Atapuerca, nicknamed 'Excalibur', discovered in the Sierra de Atapuerca near Burgos, Spain in 2003. It has been described as the world's oldest ritual artefact created by early *Homo neanderthalensis* for use in at least one funerary rite; although it might better be described as the world's oldest conspicuous ritual artefact, as there are many, far older, axes that were evidently crafted to be aesthetically pleasing for some non-utilitarian purpose.

This addition of the colour red as the colour of dusk and dawn has profound implications regarding the eschatology of these archaic communities, for the narrative they suggest is this: just as Day must become Night, so Night must become Day; and just as the Living must die, so the Dead must live again.

This interpretation is further suggested by the placement by various communities among *Homo heidelbergensis* (in the Sierra de Atapuerca, Spain) and *Homo neanderthalensis* (in Le Regourdou in the Dordogne,

France) of the remains of bears in their tombs and graves, the bears having possibly been sacrificed as part of the funeral ceremony. The bear, with its habit of disappearing from the surface world in winter to hibernate and then returning in the spring, is an obvious choice as a symbol of resurrection.

The association of life, death and resurrection with the daily cycle of night and day indicate a belief in a regular cycle of resurrection rather than a single event like the Judgement Day of Christianity. It follows then that the Netherworld was only a temporary home to the Dead. We should, however, think of it as existing in a time outside time, thus our ancestors are, from our perspective at least, always to be found there. Furthermore, as will be discussed anon, we should recognise that the Dream Realm forms part of the Netherworld.

In some cases resurrection may have been an option that was only open to a limited few, the heroes or leaders of a community. The ceremonial burial of a male *Homo sapiens* covered in red ochre thirty-three thousand years ago in the Goat's Hole cave in Wales, an individual dubbed the Red Lady of Paviland in the nineteenth century, may have been such a hero.

We might find an echo of this archaic eschatology in folklore, such as the Welsh tales in which heroes like King Arthur or Owain Glyndŵr are said to be sleeping in a cave, awaiting the time when they will awaken to fulfil their destinies. The dead are only sleeping.

We find elements of this primal cosmology in the mythology of Ancient Greece. In Greek myth the Titaness Nyx (Night) is the mother of Thanatos (Death) and his twin brother Hypnos (Sleep), whose homes lie adjacent to one another in Hades. The home of Hypnos is a cave around which flows the river Lethe (Forgetfulness), whose waters, when imbibed, cause the dead to forget their past and dreamers to forget their dreams.

According to one myth, upon death a person makes a choice to either drink from the river Lethe, the waters of Hypnos, or from the spring of memory, the waters of the Titaness Mnemosyne (Memory). Those who drink from the former forget their pain and sorrow and all they have learned in life and are reborn on earth again; while those who choose to drink from the latter go to the Elysian Fields, where there is no strife or pain.

Manifestations of the Netherworld

It is only since the advent of institutional Christianity – reinforced shortly afterwards by the advent of Islam – that the Western conception of the Underworld has become thoroughly unreal. Prior to the promotion of vast caverns filled with lakes of fire in popular culture, the Land of the Dead had always been perceived as identical to locations in the real world.

Depending on where you lived, your Hades could be a desert, a moor, a forest, mountains, marshes, the ocean, an archipelago or even that old Greek classic: a bunch of caves. Whichever it would be, it was always somewhere with a real life representation in your own neighbourhood or region.

In an urban setting the most obvious representation of the Netherworld is the graveyard. The renowned

Texan magician Professor Charles Porterfield describes graveyards as being 'embassies of the Underworld', in that they form part of the Netherworld in the same way that the embassy of a nation, though located abroad, is still part of the nation it represents. If we apply the maxim *Nox Infernus Est*, then at nightfall the graveyard changes from being an embassy of the Underworld to being its very centre.

Dream

The Dead appear to be sleeping and Sleepers appear to be dead. The superficial resemblance between the two conditions is arguably the foundation upon which the connection between Night and the Netherworld was built in the minds of archaic humans. However, the connection between Dream and afterlife realms is far from being merely a symbolic and imaginary one.

Contrary to the views of scientism and psychiatry, dreams are not an individual's private sandbox. In dreams we can be visited by spirits, including gods, other dreamers, and the spirits of the Dead.

When we are awake we can easily distinguish our external reality from our internal thoughts and imaginings, but in Dream there is no clear division between the two; that is to say, in any same scenario within a dream we might see the products of our own minds and at the same time encounter spirits and locations that are not imagined but exist independently. In some instances we might find ourselves for all intents and purposes fully awake inside solid, physically tactile locations within Dream. This division between the imagined and the real was referred to in Classical Antiquity as the Gates of Horn and Ivory: true visions were entered through the Gates of Horn, while the Gates of Ivory only led to fantasies.

It is beyond the scope of this prospectus to list the realms and experiences that can be accessed in Dream as they have no known limit, and almost all assertions attempting to place a limit on what dreamers can do are erroneous.

If we think of Dream as an interface, it is one that is receptive to programming, which the dreamer can do prior to going to sleep. There are multiple ways to program dreams, such as asking our spirit allies to send certain dreams, summoning spirits to our dreams through incantations or prayer, or by placing charms or amulets or other objects related to our desired dream experience under our pillows. All such methods can be improvised.

The student of the Wandering School should expect to be visited in dreams by all manner of spirits, and bear in mind that, apart from the spirits of personal acquaintances, spirits will often come in the guise of celebrities and TV or movie characters who best represent those spirits. Even when this is not the case, they will more than likely appear in modern apparel rather than in the clothes of a bygone era.

Dreaming like Rhonabwy

In the Welsh tale *Breuddwyd Rhonabwy* (*The Dream of Rhonabwy*) Prince Madog ap Maredudd, the twelfth century ruler of Powys, sends Rhonabwy and two companions to find the prince's rebellious brother Iorwertth.

One night during the pursuit they seek shelter with Heilyn the Red, but find his longhouse filthy and his beds full of fleas. Lying down on a yellow ox-skin, Rhonabwy experiences a dream in which he meets and converses with King Arthur.

Some might ponder the mythological significance of a yellow ox-skin and the role it might play in facilitating magical dreams and visions, but any student who has occasion to sleep out in the cold with only the coat or jacket they happen to be wearing to keep warm will learn that the key to Rhonabwy's dream-vision is discomfort.

This discomfort induces what could be best described as a half-sleep, by which we do not mean simply 'light sleeping,' but a state of consciousness which hovers between being asleep and being awake.

In this between state, student will find themselves conversing with spirits. These conversations may form part of a vision located in another place, as occurs in Rhonabwy's case, but often they will take place in the real world location we happen to be in – not imagined but viewed with half-open eyes. These spirits are often local ones, but on other occasions they might be companion spirits such as ancestral guardians or familiars.

Obviously, some locations are potentially more interesting than others, such as haunted houses, ancient burial chambers, pagan shrines and so on. But an entity will likely be met regardless of location.

It should go without saying that this should not be attempted in adverse climatic conditions.

VII

SEPTEM SUNT

Recent translations of medieval grimoires have shown just how integral certain aspects of astrology were to medieval magic. There is the use of electional astrology in the creation of talismans such as in the *Picatrix*; there is the use of horary astrology in divination; there is the use of astrology in medicine; there is the use of planetary hours in Solomonic and folk magic; and there is the use of astrological correspondences in geomancy. Some of these practices require the use of actual astrology, while others do not. What they all have in common is that they revolve around the Seven Planetary Spirits.

It has been suggested by some notable magicians, particularly Jake Stratton-Kent, that the Seven Spirits most likely predate their astrological correspondence with the seven traditional planets. They may have their origins in a combination of the three stations of the Sun (sunrise, noon, and sunset) with the four seasons or the four directions; or the four winds, or some similar combination; and in Goetia we have an infernal set of seven spirits by combining the three chiefs Lucifer, Beelzebub, and Astaroth with the Four Kings. Nevertheless, the seven planetary gods date back to Ancient Mesopotamia, the first recognisably organised system of astrology emerging in Babylonia c. 1800 BCE.

Babylonian priests used astrology as a system of omens to interpret the will and disposition of the seven planetary gods and did so during or shortly in advance of an astronomical event. It would not be until c. 400 BCE that astrologers could calculate and predict the movement of the planets and create the first ephemeris, by which time astrologers were already among the itinerant oriental magicians and mystics bringing their arcane traditions into Greece. Following the establishment of a Greek dynasty in Egypt, Graeco-Egyptian astrologers blended Babylonian and Egyptian astrology (which was itself very likely developed from a blend of astrological traditions, namely of Palaeolithic African star lore with the Anatolian star lore that was part and parcel of the neolithic agrarian revolution) to create what we now call Traditional Western Astrology, just as Graeco-Egyptian sorcerers blended Middle Eastern, Greek, and Egyptian magic to create the Western Tradition of magic.

Archaic astrology is possibly tens of thousands of years older, but it appears that it was not particularly interested in the planets but instead was more interested in the sun, moon, stars and the seasonal progress of another set of seven spirits, the Seven Sisters of the Pleiades, which played an important role in archaic navigation and timekeeping. Whatever the exact origin, collectively they and the number Seven represent completeness, the cosmos, time and destiny.

It is important to stress that astrology and astrological magic is fundamentally a Seven Spirit system. It has nothing to do with more recently discovered planets and both astrology and astrological magic cease to function

VII. SEPTEM SUNT

properly when non-traditional planets are added. *Septem sunt*, 'seven are they'.

From the period known as the Enlightenment through to the late twentieth century, Western astrologers attempted to distance astrology from magic and present it as something more scientific, an objectively real science. During this period new planets were discovered and astrologers adopted them, thereby confusing astrology with astronomy and throwing a spanner in the works. During the same period we saw the advent of psychology which astrologers and occultists alike used to replace Spirit.

In traditional astrology and astrological magic there are seven planets, period. Engaging with new planets and attributing meaning to them activates them magically, and to no good end: they are an unnecessary complication, particularly in astrological magic. In the interpretation of horoscopes, any event attributed to the new planets can be explained without their presence by any astrologer worth their salt.

By adding modern astronomical phenomena (such as new planets) in the mistaken belief that traditional astrology is simply outdated astronomy, the modern astrologer misses the point entirely and undermines the working magical foundation of astrology.

Furthermore, engaging with the new planets magically, such as in the creation of talismans, is dangerous to the individual who does so. They are, by virtue of their invisibility to the naked eye, wholly malefic, with natures not unlike those of the dreadful Old Ones in the fiction of H.P. Lovecraft.

Today it is necessary to distinguish astrology from magic, and astrologers from astrological magicians. Historically this was not the case. Astrology is a system of magic, even when it is only used to forecast the future.[7] In Classical Antiquity, astrologers were very much part of the itinerant milieu of sorcerers and seers. When sorcerers were expulsed or executed en masse as occasionally would happen under Roman rule, astrologers were among them. The Islamic astrologers who reintroduced astrology into Europe were all magicians, as were its practitioners in medieval Christendom.

THE SEVEN PATRONS

The word 'planet' derives from the Greek for 'wanderer', and as wanderers they are naturally the patrons and professors of the Wandering School.

Luna

The spirit of the Moon and ruler of Monday and the sign of Cancer. In Babylonian astrology the deity associated with the Moon is not a goddess but a god, the moon-god Sin. The Akkadian-speaking Babylonians employed Sumerian as their liturgical language, much like Latin, Coptic, and old Slavonic are still used as liturgical languages today, and so Sin was also known among Babylonians by his old Sumerian name, Nanna.

---

[7] We recommend that students who wish to study astrology should consult William Lilly's *Christian Astrology* or Demetra George's *Ancient Astrology in Theory and Practice*.

He is the patron of cattle herders and boats, and one of several gods who act as judges of the dead. His consort is Nikkal, known in Sumerian as Ningal, the 'Great Queen', and they are the parents of Ishtar (Venus) and the sun-god Shamash.

In Greek astrology, the Moon is the Titaness Selene, who is equated with the Roman moon-goddess Luna. Although Luna had her own cult and temple, she was sometimes an aspect or epithet of other lunar goddesses, such as Diana, Juno, Proserpina, and Hecate. As Juno, the calends (first day) of each month is sacred to her.

According to the *Picatrix* the magician should seek from Luna 'all things pertaining to her and attributed to her nature, such as those who petition kings, urban and rural tenants, halfbreeds, messengers sent by land or sea, farm labourers, ploughmen, geometricians, stewards, portraitists, mariners and those who do work pertaining to water, the populace in general, geomancers, fiancées, the wives of kings, youths without beards, and the like.'[8]

The Latin and English hymns given on the following pages are translations of the Orphic hymn to Selene. A common practice among twenty-first century sorcerers and one that has been used at least as far back as Renaissance Italy is to recite those of the Orphic hymns that are addressed to the gods of the seven planets. It should be noted that these hymns were not composed with astrology in mind, and that the *Picatrix* supplies its readers with its own planetary prayers for use in magic; nevertheless the precedent for the use of Orphic hymns

---

8 John Michael Greer and Christopher Warnock, trans., *The Complete Picatrix* (Renaissance Astrology 2010), p. 155.

was set centuries ago. These can be used as part of a planetary-related magical working, but more commonly they are used as an offering to the planetary ruler of the day in order to maintain good relations with the planets and thereby assure their assistance when it is needed in a working.

Lunae Hymnus
Audi dea regina, lucifera, diva Luna
Tauricornis Mene, noctu currens, aerivaga,
Nocturna, facitenens, puella, bene stellata, Luna,
Quae crescis et decrescis, foeminaque et mas
Fulgens, equorum amatrix, temporis mater, fructifera,
Electris, iracunda, splendoris causa nocturna
Omnispica, vigiliarum amatrix, pulchris syderibus abundans,
Quiete gaudens et delectatione beatifica,
Lucida, laetitiae datrix, perfectrix noctis oblectamentum
Astritenens, latipeple, vagi cursus, sapientissima puella
Venias beata, benivola, pulchristella, lumine tuo
Micans, conservans tuos supplices, proba puella.[9]

Hymn to The Moon
Hear, Goddess queen, diffusing silver light,
Bull-horn'd and wand'ring thro' the gloom of Night.
With Stars surrounded, and with circuit wide
Night's torch extending, thro' the heav'ns you ride:
Female and Male with borrow'd rays you shine,
And now full-orb'd, now tending to decline,
Mother of ages, fruit-producing Moon,

---
[9] Ilana Klutstein, *Marsilio Ficino et la Theologie Ancienne* (Leo S. Olschki Editore 1987), p. 65.

Whose amber orb makes Night's reflected noon:
Lover of horses, splendid, queen of Night,
All-seeing pow'r bedeck'd with starry light.
Lover of vigilance, the foe of strife,
In peace rejoicing, and a prudent life:
Fair lamp of Night, its ornament ad friend,
Who giv'st to Nature's works their destin'd end.
Queen of the stars, all-wise Diana hail!
Deck'd with a graceful robe and shining veil;
Come, blessed Goddess, prudent, starry, bright,
come moony-lamp with chaste and splendid light,
Shine on these sacred rites with prosp'rous rays,
And pleas'd accept thy suppliant's mystic praise.[10]

Mars

The spirit of Mars and ruler of Tuesday and the signs of Aries and Scorpio. In Babylonian astrology the planet Mars corresponds to the Sumerian god Nergal, god of war, who inflicted death and disease. He is ruler of the Underworld and, in some myths, his consort is Ereshkigal, goddess of the Underworld. The Akkadian god of plagues, Erra, was assimilated with Nergal. Together with Marduk (Jupiter) and Nabu (Mercury), Nergal was one of the Babylonian's three most important deities.

Greek astrologers in turn associated the planet with the war-god Ares, and subsequently with the Roman war-god Mars.

---

10 Thomas Taylor trans., *Orphic Hymns and Initiations* (Prometheus Trust 2003), p. 41.

According to the *Picatrix* the magician should seek from Mars 'what is consistent with his nature, such as petitions against soldiers, officials, fighters, and those who busy themselves with warlike acts, and on behalf of friends of kings, and those who destroy homes and citizens, and do evil to humanity, killers, executioners, those who work with fire, or in places such as stables, litigators, shepherds, thieves, companions on the road, liars, traitors and the like. Similarly, ask him concerning infirmities of the body from the groin downwards, phlebotomy (medical bloodletting), accumulation of gas and the like.'[11]

Martis Hymnus
Infrangibilis, magnanime, magnipotens, fortis daemon,
Armis gaudens, mortalicida, muripercussor,
Mars rex, dolisone, nece infectus semper
Sanguine peremptorum gaudens, bello conturbans, horrende,
Qui desideras ensibusque et lanceis pugnam inconcinnam
Firma contentionem rabidam, remitte laborem dolore animum afficientem,
Ad desiderium autem annue Veneris crapulasque Lyaei
Permutans fortitudinem armorum in opera Cereris
Pacem desiderans almam, faelicitatis datricem.[12]

Hymn to Mars
Magnanimous, unconquered, boisterous Mars,
in darts rejoicing, and in bloody wars
Fierce and untamed, whose mighty power can make

---

11 Greer & Warnock, *The Complete Picatrix*, p. 155.
12 Klutstein, *Marsilio Ficino et la Theologie Ancienne*, p. 98.

VII. SEPTEM SUNT

the strongest walls from their foundations shake:
Mortal destroying king, defiled with gore,
pleased with war's dreadful and tumultuous roar:
Thee, human blood, and swords, and spears delight,
and the dire ruin of mad savage fight.
Stay, furious contests, and avenging strife,
whose works with woe, embitter human life;
To lovely Venus, and to Bacchus yield,
to Ceres give the weapons of the field;
Encourage peace, to gentle works inclined,
and give abundance, with benignant mind.[13]

Mercury

The spirit of Mercury and ruler of Wednesday and the signs Gemini and Virgo. In Babylonian astrology the planet Mercury is associated with Nabu, the god of literacy, the rational arts, scribes, and wisdom. Nabu was a Semitic god worshipped by Babylonians and Assyrians, and the meaning of his name, sometimes rendered as 'announcer' in English, is cognate with the Arabic and Hebrew words for 'prophet'. He was the son of Marduk, the most powerful of the Babylonian deities, but as a god of oracles Nabu was sometimes associated with the moon-god Sin.

In Babylonian astrology Mercury was initially associated with the Sumerian god Ninurta, but as Nabu's father Marduk replaced Enlil as the chief deity. Nabu took over as the deity corresponding to the planet Mercury, keeping the lunar aspects he had been

---

13 Taylor, *Orphic Hymns and Initiations*, p. 130.

given through his association with Sin, thus the son of Enlil was replaced by the son of Marduk in the role of Mercury. Ninurta would henceforth be associated with the planet Saturn.

Greek astrologers in turn also gave this role to a son of their chief deity: Hermes, the son of Zeus. Hermes is the herald of the gods, a trickster and a guide of souls entering the Underworld. He was the protector of messengers, travellers, thieves, merchants, and orators. He was syncretised by Graeco-Egyptians with the Egyptian god of scribes, Thoth, which led to his reinvention in Late Antiquity as Hermes Trismegistos, the founder of Hermeticism and patron of magicians.

The Romans equated Hermes with the god Mercurius, better known to us as Mercury, who is the god of financial gain, commerce, eloquence, messages, communication (including divination), travellers, boundaries, luck, trickery, and thieves; he also serves as the guide of souls to the underworld, a guide in dreams, and the messenger of the gods.

According to the *Picatrix* the magician should seek from Mercury 'petitions appropriate to notaries, scribes, arithmeticians, geometers, astrologers, grammarians, lecturers, philosophers, rhetoricians, poets, sons of kings, secretaries of kings, halfbreeds, merchants, minstrels, lawyers, servants, boys, girls, younger brothers, painters, designers, and those similar to them.'[14]

---

14 Greer & Warnock, *The Complete Picatrix*, p. 155.

VII. SEPTEM SUNT

MERCURII HYMNUS
Audi me, Mercuri, Iovis nuncie, Maiae fili,
Omnipotentem animum habens, certaminum preses, princeps mortalium,
Benivole, varii consilii, executor, Argi interfector
Talarivole, amator virorum, orationis propheta mortalibus,
Gymnasiis gaudens et dolosis deceptionibus, tropheis presidens,
Interpres omnium, lucrimercator, curarum solutor
Qui manibus tenes pacis telum haud illaudandum,
Coryciota, beate, valde iuvans, varii sermonis,
Operationibus auxiliator, amice mortalibus in necessitatibus
Linguae vehemens telum venerandum hominibus:
Audi me precantem, vitae finem bonam prebens
In operationibus, orationis gratia et memoria.[15]

HYMN TO MERCURY
Hermes, draw near, and to my pray'r incline,
Angel of Jove and Maia's son divine;
Studious of contests, ruler of mankind,
With heart almighty, and a prudent mind.
Celestial messenger, of various skill,
Whose pow'rful arts could watchful Argus kill:
With winged feet, 'tis thine thro' air to course,
O friend of man, and prophet of discourse:
Great life-supporter, to rejoice is thine,
In arts gymnastic, and in fraud divine:
With pow'r endu'd all language to explain,
Of care the loos'ner, and the source of gain.
Whose hand contains of blameless peace the rod,
Corucian, blessed, profitable God;

---
15 Klutstein, *Marsilio Ficino et la Theologie Ancienne*, p. 77.

Of various speech, whose aid in works we find,
And in necessities to mortals kind:
Dire weapon of the tongue, which men revere,
Be present, Hermes, and thy suppliant hear;
Assist my works, conclude my life with peace,
Give graceful speech, and me memory's increase.[16]

Jupiter

The spirit of the planet Jupiter and ruler of Thursday and the signs of Sagittarius and Pisces. In Babylonian astrology the planet Jupiter corresponds to the god Marduk. The name Marduk is believed to derive from the Sumerian *amar utuk*, 'the bull-calf of the sun-god Utu'. He began as a minor deity, rising to prominence in the first millenium BCE to become the chief deity of the Babylonian pantheon.

Greek astrologers in turn associated the planet Jupiter with the chief deity of their own pantheon, Zeus, and he was subsequently associated with his Roman equivalent, Jupiter. Both Zeus and Jupiter are protectors of travellers and punish those who fail to be hospitable to travellers and strangers. Romans would make offerings to Jupiter in exchange for a successful journey. The Ides of each month is sacred to Jupiter.

According to the *Picatrix* the magician should seek from Jupiter 'all that belongs to his portion, such as petitions concerning sublime men, the powerful, prelates, sages, preachers of religion, judges, virtuous men, interpreters of dreams, hermits, philosophers,

---

16 Taylor, *Orphic Hymns and Initiations*, p. 72.

kings, their sons, the children of their sons, (royal) soldiers, and (royal) cousins; petitions for peace and profit; and anything similar may be sought from him.'[17]

Iovis Hymnus
Iuppiter valde honorande, incorruptibilis, hoc tibi nos
Testimonium reddimus liberatorium et votum.
O rex, per tuum caput apparuere haec facile
Terra dea mater montiumque altisona iuga
Et pontus et omnia, quaecunque coelum intus ordine continet.
Iuppiter saturnie, sceptritenens, descensor, magnanime
Omniparens, principium omnium omniumque finis,
Concussor terrae, auctor, purgator, omnia quatiens,
Fulgurator, tonans, fulminator, native Iuppiter
Audi me, diversiformis, daque salubritatem inculpabilem
Pacemque deam et divitiarum gloriam iustam.[18]

Hymn to Jupiter
O Jove much-honor'd, Jove supremely great,
To thee our holy rites we consecrate,
Our pray'rs and expiations, king divine,
For all things round thy head exalted shine.
The earth is thine, and mountains swelling high,
The sea profound, and all within the sky.
Saturnian king, descending from above,
Magnanimous, commanding, sceptred Jove;
All-parent, principle and end of all,
Whose pow'r almighty, shakes this earthly ball;
Ev'n Nature trembles at thy mighty nod,

---
17 Greer & Warnock, *The Complete Picatrix*, pp. 154-155.
18 Klutstein, *Marsilio Ficino et la Theologie Ancienne*, p. 69.

Loud-sounding, arm'd with light'ning, thund'ring God.
Source of abundance, purifying king,
O various-form'd from whom all natures spring;
Propitious hear my pray'r, give blameless health,
With peace divine, and necessary wealth.[19]

Venus

Spirit of the planet Venus and ruler of Friday and the signs of Taurus and Libra. In Babylonian astrology the corresponding deity is the goddess Ishtar, also known by her Sumerian name Inanna. Inanna seems to have begun as a goddess of fertility and the harvest of the fruit of the date palm before becoming the goddess of love and war as well as fertility. Her consort was the divine herdsman Dumuzid, and both have varying myths related to resurrection following a journey to the Underworld. Her most prominent epithet is 'Queen of Heaven' and she is able to intercede on a supplicant's behalf with any deity in any matter.

Greek astrologers in turn associated this planet with Aphrodite, goddess of love, lust, beauty, pleasure, passion, and procreation; and subsequently with her Roman equivalent, Venus, goddess of love, sex, desire, beauty, prosperity, and victory.

According to the *Picatrix* the magician should seek from Venus 'all things that pertain to her, such as petitions of women, boys, and girls, and daughters, and generally everything pertaining to the love of women and carnal copulation with them, art, vocal and

---

19 Taylor, *Orphic Hymns and Initiations*, p. 56.

instrumental music, telling jokes, and all those who give themselves over to worldly pleasures, those who engage in vices, male and female servants, brides and grooms, mothers, friends, sisters, and all those similar to them.'[20]

Veneris Hymnus
Coelestis, multum preconiis celebrata, ridibunda Venus,
Mari nata, genitrix dea, amatrix nocturnarum vigiliarum, veneranda,
Nocturna iugatrix, dolistructrix, mater Necessitatis.
Omnia enim ex te sunt, subiugasti autem orbem
Et imperas tribus Parcis, generas autem omnia,
Quaecunque in coelo sunt et in terra frugifera
In marique profundoque, veneranda Baccho assidens,
Gaudens conviviis et festivitatibus, nuptiarum ornatrix mater Cupidinum,
Suada gaudens cubilibus, oculta, gratiarum datrix,
Apparens latensque, desiderandae comae, bono parente nata,
Nymphica cum conviviis deorum, sceptra tenens, lupa,
Generationis datrix, amatrix virorum, desideratissima, vitae datrix,
Quae iugasti mortales infrenibus necessitatibus
Et ferarum immensum genus amorifurentibus philtris:
Veni, Cyprogenia deum genus, sive in Olympo
Es tu dea regina pulchra laeta facie,
Seu thuriferae Syriae solum frequentas,
Sive tu in campis cum curribus auristructis
Aegypti contines sacrae genitalia lavacra,
Sive et ceruleis littoribus ad marinam undam
Laeta gaudes mortalium circularibus choreis,
Sive nymphis delectaris cerulicoloribus in terra diva

---
20 Greer & Warnock, *The Complete Picatrix*, p. 155.

Delata per littora arenosa levi curru,
Sive in Cypro, regina, altrici tua, ub pulchare te
Virgines indomitae nymphaeque per totum annum
Celebrant hymnis, te, beata, et immortalem sanctum Adonin.
Veni, beata dea, pulchramabilem spetiem habens:
Animo enim te voco, veneranda, sacris orationibus.[21]

HYMN TO VENUS
Heav'nly, illustrious, laughter-loving queen,
Sea-born, night-loving, of an awful mien;
Crafty, from whom necessity first came,
Producing, nightly, all-connecting dame:
Tis thine the world with harmony to join,
For all things spring from thee, O pow'r divine.
The triple Fates are rul'd by thy decree,
And all productions yield alike to thee:
Whate'er the heav'ns, encircling all contain,
Earth fruit-producing, and the stormy main,
Thy sway confesses, and obeys thy nod,
Awful attendant of the brumal God:
Goddess of marriage, charming to the sight,
Mother of Loves, whom banquetings delight;
Source of persuasion, secret, fav'ring queen,
Illustrious born, apparent and unseen:
Spousal, lupercal, and to men inclin'd,
Prolific, most-desir'd, life-giving., kind:
Great sceptre-bearer of the Gods, 'tis thine,
Mortals in necessary bands to join;
And ev'ry tribe of savage monsters dire
In magic chains to bind, thro' mad desire.

---

21 Klutstein, *Marsilio Ficino et la Theologie Ancienne*, pp. 92-93.

VII. SEPTEM SUNT

Come, Cyprus-born, and to my pray'r incline,
Whether exalted in the heav'ns you shine,
Or pleas'd in Syria's temple to preside,
Or o'er th' Egyptian plains thy car to guide,
Fashion'd of gold; and near its sacred flood,
Fertile and fam'd to fix thy blest abode;
Or if rejoicing in the azure shores,
Near where the sea with foaming billows roars,
The circling choirs of mortals, thy delight,
Or beauteous nymphs, with eyes cerulean bright,
Pleas'd by the dusty banks renown'd of old,
To drive thy rapid, two-yok'd car of gold;
Or if in Cyprus with thy mother fair,
Where married females praise thee ev'ry year,
And beauteous virgins in the chorus join,
Adonis pure to sing and thee divine;
Come, all-attractive to my pray'r inclin'd,
For thee, I call, with holy, reverent mind.[22]

Saturn

The spirit of the planet Saturn and ruler of Saturday and the signs of Capricorn and Aquarius. In Babylonian astrology the deity corresponding to the planet Saturn is Ninib, known in Sumerian as Ninurta. Initially Ninurta was associated with the planet Mercury, but with the rise in prominence of Marduk and his son Nabu in the Babylonian pantheon, Ninurta was switched to Saturn, Originally a god of agriculture and of healing, he had become a war-god by the Babylonian era. His temple

---

22 Taylor, *Orphic Hymns and Initiations*, pp. 116-117.

staff were hired from among the poor and destitute, and one of their duties was the witnessing of documents.

The corresponding deity in Greek astrology is the titan Kronos, whose Roman equivalent is the god Saturnus, better known to us today as Saturn. He is a god of time, generation, dissolution, abundance, wealth, agriculture, periodic renewal, and liberation. His temple in Rome housed the treasury where the Roman Republic's reserves of gold and silver were stored. The state archives and the insignia and official scale for the weighing of metals were also housed there.

According to the *Picatrix* the magician should 'ask Saturn in petitions concerning old people or generous men, senators and rulers of cities, hermits, those who labour in the earth, restoration of citizenship and inheritance, distinguished men, farmers, builders of buildings, servants, thieves, fathers, grandfathers and great-grandfathers.'[23]

SATURNI HYMNUS
Semper redivive, deorum pater atque etiam hominum,
Varii consilii, immaculate, magnipotens, fortis Titan,
Qui consummis quidem omnia augesque rursus ipse,
Vincula ineffabilia qui habes per universum orbem,
Aevi Saturne totius genitor, Saturne varii consilii,
Terraeque germen et Coeli syderei,
Generationis augmen, diminutio, Opis marite, venerande Prometheus,
Qui habitas per omnes mundi partes, principiium generationis mundi,

---

23 Greer & Warnock, *The Complete Picatrix*, p. 154.

VII. SEPTEM SUNT

Curvi consilii, prestantissime: audiens supplicem vocem
Mittas valde beatum vitae finem de quo numquam queri possimus.[24]

HYMN TO SATURN
Etherial father, mighty Titan, hear,
Great fire of gods and men, whom all revere:
Endu'd with various council, pure and strong,
to whom perfection and decrease belong.
Consum'd by thee all forms that hourly die,
by thee restor'd, their former place supply;
The world immense in everlasting chains,
strong and ineffable thy pow'r contains
Father of vast eternity, divine,
O mighty Saturn, various speech is thine:
Blossom of earth and of the starry skies,
husband of Rhea, and Prometheus wife.
Obstetric Nature, venerable root,
from which the various forms of being shoot;
No parts peculiar can thy pow'r enclose,
diffus'd thro' all, from which the world arose,
O, best of beings, of a subtle mind,
propitious hear to holy pray'rs inclin'd;
The sacred rites benevolent attend,
and grant a blameless life, a blessed end.[25]

Sol

Spirit of the Sun and ruler of Sunday and the sign of Leo. In Babylonian astrology the corresponding deity

---

24 Klutstein, *Marsilio Ficino et la Theologie Ancienne*, p. 68.
25 Taylor, *Orphic Hymns and Initiations*, p. 51.

is the sun-god Shamash, whose Sumerian name is Utu. In addition to being the god of the sun, he is a god of justice and divination and he is a protector of travellers.

His Greek counterpart is the titan Helios who, in addition to being the personification of the sun, is also the ancestor of witches. His Roman counterpart is Sol.

According to the *Picatrix* the magician should seek from Sol 'those petitions that are appropriate to him, such as petitions against kings, the sons of warriors and kings, exalted people who delight in justice and truth and abhor falsehood and violence, desirous of good reputation and seeking popular acclaim, officials, clergy, physicians, philosophers, exalted people who are humble, perceptive and magnanimous, older brothers, fathers and the like.'[26]

SOLIS HYMNUS
Audi beate, omnispice habens aeternum oculum,
Titan aurimicans, Hyperion, coelestis lux,
Per te nate, indefatigabilis, animalium et iocunde aspectus,
Dexter genitor aurorae, sinister noctis,
Temperaturam habens horarum, quadrigressibus pedibus tripudians
Bone cursor, sonore, ignee, clari vultus, auriga,
Turbinis immensi versationibus iter peragens,
Piis dux bonorum, impiis inimicus,
Aureae lyrae mundi enarmonium cursum trahens,
Operum significator bonorum, montium alumne puer
Munditenens, fistula canens, ignicursor, circumvage,
Phosphore, varia ostendens, vitam afferens, fructifer Paean,

---
26 Greer & Warnock, *The Complete Picatrix*, p. 155.

VII. SEPTEM SUNT

Fervide, immaculate, temporis ala, immortalis Iupiter,
Serene, passim lucens, mundi circularis ocule,
Qui extingueris fulgesque pulchris radiis claris
Ostensor iusticiae, amator aquarum, domine mundi,
Fidel servator, semper excelsissime, omnibus auxiliator,
Ocule iustitiae, vitae lux: o equorum impulsor,
Scutica stridula quadrisublimatum currum impellens,
Audi orationes, iocundam autem vitam sacerdotibus indica.[27]

HYMN TO THE SUN
Hear, golden Titan, whose eternal eye
With matchless sight illumines all the sky.
Native, unwearied in diffusing light,
And to all eyes the object of delight:
Lord of the Seasons, beaming light from far,
Sonorous, dancing in thy four-yok'd car.
With thy right hand the source of morning light,
And with thy left the father of the night.
Agile and vig'rous, venerable Sun,
Fiery and bright around the heav'ns you run,
Foe to the wicked, but the good man's guide,
O'er all his steps propitious you preside.
With various-sounding golden lyre 'tis thine
To fill the world with harmony divine.
Father of ages, guide of prosp'rous deeds,
The world's commander, borne by lucid steeds.
Immortal Jove, flute-playing, bearing light,
Source of existence, pure and fiery bright;
Bearer of fruit, almighty lord of years,
Agile and warm, whom ev'ry power reveres.

---
27 Klutstein, *Marsilio Ficino et la Theologie Ancienne*, pp. 64-65.

Bright eye, that round the world incessant flies,
Doom'd with fair fulgid rays to set and rise;
Dispensing justice, lover of the stream,
The world's great master, and o'er all supreme.
Faithful defender, and the eye of right,
Of steeds the ruler, and of life the light:
With sounding whip four fiery steeds you guide,
When in the glittering car of day you ride,
Propitious on these mystic labours shine,
And bless thy suppliants with a life divine.[28]

PLANETARY HOURS ON THE ROAD

Calculating planetary hours can be an inconvenience while on the road. Fortunately the sorcerer can easily identify who rules the noon and sunset on any given day, so long as the sorcerer knows what day it is.

Planetary hours progress from Saturn to Jupiter to Mars to Sol to Venus to Mercury to Luna and then begin again with Saturn. The four quarters of the day, however, go in the opposite direction to the hours. Thus, if the Sun rises in the hour of Luna, then noon will be in the hour of Mercury, sunset in the hour of Venus and midnight in the hour of Sol. This makes using the four quarters of the day in connection with their planetary rulerships a far more convenient method of using planetary hours for the itinerant sorcerer.

---

28 Taylor, *Orphic Hymns and Initiations*, pp. 39-40..

VII. SEPTEM SUNT

PLANETARY **C**HORDS

The Seven Spirits can also have their corresponding musical keys. For example:

Do (C) Saturn   Sol (G) Sol
Re (D) Luna   La (A) Mars
Mi (E) Mercury   Si (B) Jupiter
Fa (F) Venus   Do (C) Saturn

THE **P**LANETARY **R**OSARY

For students who wish to combine planetary spells with the Holy Rosary.

- Lunar spells with the Joyful Mysteries on Monday mornings and Thursday evenings.
- Martian spells with the Sorrowful Mysteries on Tuesday mornings and Friday evenings.
- Mercurian spells with the Glorious Mysteries on Wednesday mornings and Saturday evenings.
- Jovian spells with the Joyful Mysteries on Thursday mornings and also, between Advent and Lent, on Sunday evenings.
- Venusian spells with the Joyful Mysteries on Monday evenings.
- Saturnian spells with the Sorrowful Mysteries on Tuesday evenings.
- Solar spells with the Glorious Mysteries on Wednesday evenings and also, between Easter and Advent, on Sunday mornings.

MUNDUS NOBIS LOQUITUR

VIII

MUNDUS NOBIS LOQUITUR

Local spirits and in particular spirits of place are as important to the sedentary sorcerer as ancestral spirits. In the indigenous cultures of Australia such spirits of place are considered to be ancestors, and the sedentary sorcerer in the West would not be mistaken in treating these spirits as such.

The itinerant student of the Wandering School, however, constantly moving from one location to another, doesn't have time to establish long-term relationships with local spirits. Nevertheless they remain an important consideration on the student's journey. When entering a town or city, the sorcerer should seek out the river and offer a coin in greeting, or else seek out a fountain which is already being used as a wishing well. A sorcerer should learn who the patron saints of a place are and where their churches are located. Legendary and historical figures are worth taking into consideration, and it will be of benefit to students to visit local graveyards and pay their respects to the local dead.

A sorcerer shines like a beacon to spirits, and so wherever the sorcerer goes, local spirits will attempt to communicate with the student, sometimes in dreams, and more often than not through synchronicities and epiphanies. Indeed, it is by these means that all gods and spirits and the Cosmos itself communicates with us. *Mundus nobis loquitur*, 'the world speaks to us'.

Synchronicities are meaningful coincidences, events which occur with no apparent causal relationship with each other yet seem to be meaningfully related. The psychiatrist Carl Gustav Jung coined the term 'synchronicity' to describe this phenomenon, which is a universally-experienced encounter with the 'paranormal'.

Synchronicities happen all the time everywhere and work through any and every medium; this includes absolutely anything that is meaningful to an individual's consciousness: fiction, astrology, symbolism, philosophy, mythology, religion, pop trivia – all inform the individual's personal experience of synchronicity.

Most of the time we only notice this phenomenon when we deliberately engage with it, which is perhaps just as well as rationalist sceptics have sometimes suffered mental breakdowns as a direct result of becoming aware of this phenomenon and subsequently experiencing an unsought-for and relentless stream of synchronicities.

There are many distinct systems or traditions of sorcery and divination, each with their own symbols, correspondences, and spirits. When a person engages with a system or tradition of magic or divination, synchronicities related to the symbolism, correspondences, and spirits of that system or tradition will be activated; and when a sorcerer arrives at a location, the narratives and symbols of the spirits of that location are also activated.

VIII. MUNDUS NOBIS LOQUITUR

As previously mentioned, spirits use synchronicities to engage and communicate with us. These synchronicities are sometimes refered to as 'epiphanies', particularly in cases where the spirits in question are deities or other entities of a divine nature. Spirits also use synchronicities to physically manifest themselves through the agency of natural and mundane phenomena, including weather (for example, a thunderclap, a sudden downpour or shaft of sunlight or gust of wind), fauna (for example, the sudden appearance or cry of an animal) and through other people (for example, an encounter with someone who coincidently embodies the spirit in question).

The aforementioned use by synchronicity of anything that may be meaningful to an individual mind is one of the reasons why students need to familiarise themselves both with mythology and with the symbols and correspondences of whichever magical system they choose to employ, in order to filter out the dross of trivia and fine-tune their communication with the Cosmos. To that end we shall list some recommended texts in the next chapter.

DIVINATION

Another way to communicate with spirits and with the Cosmos is by way of divination. There are many forms of divination, including casting runes, Chinese fortune sticks, the *I Ching*, medieval geomancy, horary astrology, scrying, bibliomancy, various forms of cartomancy such as with playing cards, Tarot, the Petit Lenormand, and these are only the more commonly known among countless forms of divination. Students may choose to employ any form of divination they wish to, but we make two recommendations: firstly, a deck of playing cards (a.k.a. 'the Devil's picture book'), as these are inconspicuous and yet give direct and unvarnished answers; secondly, if the student wishes to pay their way as a fortune teller while on their journey, they should do so using the Tarot, as this is what the majority of their potential customers will want and expect.

IX

LEGENDA DEOS EVIGILAT

During the performance of certain conjurations, a Solomonic magician will claim to be King Solomon in order to exert authority over the spirits being conjured. Some mages believe the spirits are easily fooled and thus are unable to distinguish the magician from the legendary king, but such suppositions are entirely erroneous. It is instead an example of the important role of mythological narrative in conjuration. *Legenda deos evigilat*, 'the legend awakens the gods'.

Whether we are Solomonic mages claiming to be Solomon, or Welsh bards claiming to be Taliesin, we are transposing the mythic onto ourselves. It is not about 'fooling' spirits – those spirits form part of the myth being transposed. We engage with them by entering their story.

When we celebrate holidays such as Easter and Christmas, we are transposing the mythic onto the calendar. When we 'awaken' the spirit of an artefact or imbue an object with spirit, we are transposing the mythic onto that object. In the section on manifestations of the Netherworld in Chapter VI we discussed how local woods, marshes, or caves might be considered physical representations of the Netherworld. These are examples of the transposition of the mythic onto a location.

Whether we transpose the mythic onto a place, an object, a date or a person, we are essentially engaging in an activity that all children are familiar with, usually referred to as 'make believe' and which these days more often than not is inspired by modern works of fiction rather than mythology. A stick might be a Jedi laser sword, a cave might be the entrance to an Indiana Jones adventure; a forest track might lead to the heart of Mirkwood or Lothlorien; and every wardrobe might be a portal to Narnia.

Immersing oneself in myth and legend is, therefore, important in the performance of magic. It is also, as mentioned in the previous chapter, beneficial to the fine-tuning of synchronicities; students who familiarise themselves with these tales will acquire their own mental database of mythological correspondences. Additionally, mythology connects us to our ancestors and the sorcerers of the past, acting as a common frame of reference and symbolic language through which they can communicate with us. Students should therefore begin to familiarise themselves with such tales before they begin attending the Wandering School. In familiarising themselves with a mythological entity, students should note its story, its lore, its correspondences, its relationships with other entities, and its family tree.

Students should have at least one mythological work in their possession while on the road; we recommend between one and three works. We present here our list of recommended works as a blueprint for the student's consideration. We focus primarily on works that form part of the European Dreamtime.

The term 'Dreamtime' was coined by anthropologists and is not a literal or correct rendering of any terms used in the indigenous languages of Australia, nevertheless it, along with the term 'Dreaming', has been adopted by Aboriginals themselves as useful terms to express pan-aboriginal concepts.

It should be understood that these terms are not directly concerned with dreams. Instead, the reason Aboriginals adopted these terms is that the word 'dream' conveys the liminality, otherness, and mythic nature of these concepts.

Dreamtime is circular, recurring time; it is the time of myths which is both past and ever-present, ever-recurring, eternal. The Dreamtime is where the legendary lives, where myths are ongoing events; and so the myths and legends of European heritage form part of the European Dreamtime.

Primary Texts

These are divided into three categories. We recommend that the student be in possession of physical copies of a maximum one book from each category, and as an absolute minimum one book from one of these categories.

1. The Old Abrahamic Sacred Texts.

In this category we find the Hebrew Bible, Christian Bibles and the Quran. We qualify them here as 'old' to distinguish them from more recent Abrahamic sacred texts such as the *Book of Mormon* and the *Kitab-i-Aqdas*.

The Bible is the foundational sacred text of Christianity, Christian mythology and also of the European grimoire tradition as well as various folk magic traditions of Europe and the Americas. The Hebrew Bible or Old Testament is, needless to say, the fundamental sacred text in Judaism, Jewish mythology, and Jewish magic. The same is true of the Quran in Islam. Catholic Bibles include the *Apocrypha* which includes the Book of Tobit in which the archangel Raphael plays an important role. Bibles can be used in bibliomancy, which we will speak more of below. Bibles and Qurans come in all shapes and sizes and so small, more portable editions are recommended for the journey with the Wandering School.

2. Classical Mythology

In this category we find the mythology of Greece and Rome. Greek works include Hesiod's *Theogony*, Homer's *Iliad* and *Odyssey*, and various versions of the *Argonautica*. Roman works include Virgil's *Aeneid* and Ovid's *Metamorphoses*. It is worth noting that Renaissance Italians were fond of using the *Aeneid* in bibliomancy.

As in the case of the Bible and the Quran, there are various editions of each of these works available. They are fundamental works of mythology in the collective heritage of Europe and the West.

3. Medieval Mythology

In this category we find works of mythology composed in medieval Europe, both pagan and Christian, such as the Icelandic *Eddas*, the German

IX. LEGENDA DEOS EVIGILAT

Heroic Sagas, the Welsh *Book of Taliesin*, works of Irish mythology such as the *Táin Bó Cúailnge*, and other works such as the *Testament of Solomon*, legends of Alexander the Great, Arthurian works such as *Le Morte d'Arthur* and the hagiographies of the *Legenda aurea* or Golden Legend. We also include in this category nineteenth century compilations of medieval tales such as the Welsh *Mabinogion* or of old oral legends such as the Fimmish *Kalavela*, the German folktales collected by the Brothers Grimm, and the collection of Mediterranean, Arabian and Persian tales known as *The Arabian Nights* or *1001 Nights*.

Secondary Texts

If the student has not yet reached the recommended maximum of three books from those listed above, they may wish to take one of the following books along with them on their journey. These works are divided into four categories.

1. Ancient Mythology

The oldest recorded myths in the world are those of Mesopotamia and Egypt, and these two civilisations also happen to be the grandparents of the Western Tradition of magic. We can recommend the following publications: *Myths from Mesopotamia: Creation, The Flood, Gilgamesh and Others*, translated by Stephanie Dalley; *Enheduana: The Complete Poems of the World's First Author* by Sophus Helle; *Treasure of Darkness: A History of Mesopotamian Religion* by Thorkild Jacobsen; *Myths and*

Legends of Ancient Egypt by Lewis Spence; and *The Ancient Egyptian Books of the Afterlife* by Erik Horning.

2. Classical Histories

In this category we find such Greek and Roman works as Pliny the Elder's *Natural History*, Ovid's *Fasti* and the *Histories* of Herodotus; works containing the stories the people of antiquity told themselves about themselves and the world they lived in and which preserve much information concerning folklore, legends, and pagan religious customs. We might add to this category the *Corpus Hermetica* as well as *The Golden Ass* and *Aesop's Fables*.

3. Early Modern and Modern Mythology.

In this category we find works which through their impact and continuing influence upon culture have become part of the European Dreamtime. These include the works of Shakespeare, Milton's *Paradise Lost*, the *Don Quijote* of Cervantes and Goethe's *Faust*.

4. Modern Sacred Texts.

Most modern sacred texts such as the *Book of Mormon*, the *Bayan* and the *Kitab-i-Aqdas* do not form part of the European Dreamtime, but works such as *Liber AL vel Legis* and the *Satanic Bible* have at least permeated European occulture and, needless to say, are essential texts for Thelemites and Satanists just as the *Book of Mormon* and the *Bayan* are for Mormons and Bayanis. We might also add to this category certain works of fiction such as the Cthulhu Mythos of HP Lovecraft,

Chambers' *The King in Yellow*, the *Principia Discordia* and even *The Silmarillion*.

BIBLIOMANCY

Bibliomancy is a form of divination where a question is answered by randomly picking a verse from a book. The Bible, the Quran, the works of Homer and Virgil's *Aeneid* are all known to have been used for this purpose. Generally, the larger the book and the more diverse its contents, the better. In that regard the complete works of Shakespeare would be far superior to, for example, *Liber AL vel Legis*.

The student should be wary, however, of asking a book for advice. Each book has its own spirit and character rooted in the era of its composition and will give advice according to the nature and character of that period, which may result in bad advice for the modern day magician. Seek advice elsewhere.

X
REX INFERNIS MUNDUM REGIT

The Rector of the Wandering School of Secrets is the Devil.

Students will most likely be familiar with the Christian portrayal of the Devil: a figure who is the personification of evil; the author of sin; the angel who rebelled against God. However, on closer inspection it soon becomes apparent that this figure encompasses many distinct entities, such as Lucifer, Beelzebub, Satan, Mephistopheles, and Veles; and many distinct roles, such as the Evil One, the Adversary, the Tempter, the Punisher of Sin, the Author of Sin, the Lord of this World, the Trickster, and the Master of Witchcraft; the latter three of these best describe the Devil in his role as Rector of the Wandering School

It is no accident that the archetype of a divine or supernatural trickster – be it in the form of Pan, Hermes, Veles, or the Devil of European folklore – is the patron of professional itinerants, such as troubadours, travelling craftsmen, herdsmen, merchants, tramps and entertainers, to name but a few. All life attempts to adapt to and manipulate the environment in order to survive. Another word for this manipulation is 'trickery', which encompasses all endeavours to survive by any species. For this reason the Trickster is master of all wild things as well as all human endeavours to manipulate reality.

The Slavic god Velesor Volos is perhaps one of the best representations of the Horned Trickster in pagan European mythology and folklore, as he is patron of hunters, farmers, merchants, thieves, musicians, magicians, and travellers. In the folklore of Christian Europe, the Horned Trickster became the Devil, whose folk Christian attribution as Lord of This World is in keeping with his role as patron of all human endeavour. It should therefore be evident that the Devil of the Wandering School is not the Adversary of Man and Creation, but rather their champion – albeit a terrifying, amoral, and sinister one.

In order to better familiarise ourselves with this character there are two pagan deities we should consider: the Slavic god Veles and the Greek god Pan.

VELES

Veles or Volos is referred to seven times in the Russian Primary Chronicle as a god of cattle and peasants who punishes oath-breakers with disease. He was a major Slavic deity and evidence of his cult can be found throughout the Slavic territories. He is the patron of cattle, fields, crops, forests, marshes, caves, willows, wild animals, lowlands, roads, travellers, towns, markets, commerce, merchants, poetry, troubadours, thieves, trickery, magic, earth, and water. He is god of the Netherworld, which the Slavs thought of as a sylvan marshland.

He appears in the form of a strong, young man with antlers or horns wearing a bear pelt; as an old herdsman with a long white beard, holding the staff of a pastor; as a bear, wolf, elk, owl, serpent, and as a dragon.

As a horned king of the Netherworld who also assumes the form of a dragon, it is unsurprising that he was syncretised with the Christian devil, but due to his many positive and popular attributes he was also syncretised with several Christian saints, most notably Saint Blaise.

PAN

Pan is the god of the wild, patron of shepherds, flocks, and rustic music. He is the god of fields, groves, woodlands and glens, and companion of the nymphs. His homeland is Arcadia. He is a god of fertility, sex, and springtime. In appearance he is a satyr or faun: his upper body is that of a man with goat horns while below the navel he has the hindquarters, legs, and hooves of a goat. He was worshipped in natural settings such as caves and grottoes. His corresponding equivalent in Roman mythology is the god Faunus.

Pan is famous for his sexual prowess and is often depicted with a phallus. He is an erotic trickster who used deception to seduce, among others, the moon goddess Selene.

Like Veles, however, Pan is much more than a mischievous rustic spirit. For the authors of the *Orphic Hymns* he was very much the Lord of the World:

Orphic Hymn to Pan

Strong pas'tral Pan, with suppliant voice call,
Heav'n, sea, and earth, the mighty queen of all,
Immortal fire; for all the world is thine,
And all are parts of thee, O pow'r divine.
Come, blessed Pan, whom rural haunts delight,
Come, leaping, agile, wand'ring, starry light.
Thron'd with the Seasons, Bacchanalian Pan,
Goat-footed, horn'd, from whom the world began,
Whose various parts, by thee inspir'd, combine
In endless dance and melody divine.
In thee a refuge from our fears we find,
Those fears peculiar to the humankind.
Thee, shepherds, streams of water, goats rejoice;
Thou lov'st the chase and Echo's secret voice:
The sportive Nymphs thy ev'ry step attend,
And all thy works fulfill their destin'd end.
O all-producing pow'r, much-fam'd, divine,
The world's great ruler, rich increase is thine.
All-fertile Paean, heavenly splendour pore,
In fruits rejoicing, and in caves obscure.
True serpent-horned Jove, whose dreadful rage,
When rous'd, 'tis hard for mortals to assuage.
By thee the earth wide-bosom'd deep and long,
Stands on a basis permanent and strong.
Th' unwearied waters of the rolling sea,
Profoundly spreading, yield to thy decree.
Old Ocean too reveres thy high command,
Whose liquid arms begirt the solid land.
The spacious air, whose nutrimental fire,
And vivid blasts, the heat of life inspire

X. REX INFERNIS MUNDUM REGIT

The lighter frame of fire, whose sparkling eye
Shines on the summit of the azure sky,
Submit alike to thee, whole general sway
All parts of matter, various form'd obey.
All nature's change thro' thy protecting care,
And all mankind thy lib'ral bounties share:
For these where'er dispers'd thro' boundless space,
Still find thy providence support their race.
Come, Bacchanalian, blessed power draw near,
Fanatic Pan, thy humble supplicant hear,
Propitious to these holy rites attend,
And grant my life may meet a prosp'rous end;
Drive panic Fury too, wherever found,
From humankind, to earth's remotest bound.[29]

By combining the character and attributes of Veles and Pan we acquire a fully-formed Devil as Horned Trickster, Infernal Dragon, and Lord of the World; a being both benevolent and malevolent, divine and profane. *Rex infernum mundum regit*, 'the King of Hell rules the world'.

---

29 Taylor, *Orphic Hymns and Initiations*, pp. 47-48.

XI

FORUM, FERIA ET PASTURA

While attending the Wandering School, students are expected to support themselves financially through the practice of certain professions of which the Devil as Veles and Pan is patron.

There are three theatres of operations in this respect: *forum, feria, et pastura*, the market, the fair, and the pasture.

Forum (the market) refers to market places and shopping streets. Here students seek to earn money on the street and in the market place as a street performer or street vendor. Many towns and cities require performers and vendors to apply and pay for permits to do this, which is rarely a desirable or convenient circumstance for an itinerant, and in some places these activities are not permitted at all, so students may have to run the gauntlet of avoiding the authorities. Magic will often be required to assist the student in this pursuit. Students should try their hand at being a street musician or busker, a performer of magical tricks or illusionist, a fortune teller, or an artisan selling their wares. These are all professions that the student can begin without any experience. Necessity will furnish students with sufficient motive to improve and expand their repertoires, but at the beginning the busker only needs one song, the illusionist one trick, and the artisan or vendor one product in order to ply their new trade.

XI. FORUM, FERIA ET PASTURA

Performers with large enough repertoires may find bars or cafés whose owners or managers are willing to pay them to perform on their premises; similarly, vendors with sufficient wares and resources may pay to set up a stall in a market or flea market. Students are not prohibited from doing so, so long as they continue on their journey afterwards. There is no set limit as to how long students tarry in one location; this is left to the discretion of the student.

Feria (the fair) refers here to two things: firstly, the travelling fairground or circus, and in the context of the Wandering School it refers specifically to those that include the same or similar occupations as those of the *forum* and the *pastura*; secondly, the traditional annual local fairs, such as the Spanish fiesta, the Italian festa, and the French fête. These are hubs for travelling performers, vendors, and fortune tellers. Traditionally these fairs celebrate the feast day of a location's patron saint, and in some regions one town's fair will be followed the next week by a fair in a neighbouring town, which in turn will be followed by a fair in another neighbouring town, and so students will want to mark these in their calendars. Collectively these fairs occur throughout the year, and so inevitably some will coincide with more ancient, pagan festivals. Whether they be pagan, Christian or both, they are rooted in a transposition of the mythic onto the calendar, as mentioned in Chapter IX, and so to the previously mentioned maxim *legenda deos evigilat* we might add *feriae legendam evigilant*, 'the fair awakens the legend'.

Both *forum* and *feria* require students to interact with the public from one location to the next, increasing the possibilities available to spirit allies to assist the magician, as mentioned in Chapter I. A significant proportion of students will be introverts, and this interaction with the public will also accustom them to dealing with people face-to-face and consequently lead to them being more assertive. A magician must be a sovereign individual.

Pastura (the pasture) refers to animal husbandry, the work of a pastor, and herbalism. Here the student will engage in animal husbandry in the role of a pastor, be it as a shepherd, a goatherd, a swineherd, or a herdsman of cattle. Such seasonal work is still available without the need of any paperwork in countries such as Portugal, Spain, France, and Italy.

Animal husbandry prepares the sorcerer for the Art of Evocation in multiple ways, particularly in the case of wild spirits, animal spirits, and lesser demons. To become the keeper of non-human beings with their own agendas, the sorcerer must learn to understand their behaviours. Healthy animals all have what could be described as strict behavioural codes which, when grasped, lend the sorcerer foresight as to how an animal will act or react in or to any given situation, allowing the magician to manipulate the beasts with increased proficiency.

Animals of a contrarian nature such as goats or swine need to be bribed regularly. There must always be something in it for them. Caring for the animals requires the magician to pay attention both to detail and action – a single moment of inattention in either can lead to catastrophe.

As mammals ourselves we can more easily establish a bond of sympathy with other mammals than is the case with non-mammals. In that sense, domesticated species of mammals could be described as 'Non-Human Lite'.

When working as pastors, students should seek to familiarise themselves with local herblore. Herbs have always been used in magic, and local herblore will often furnish students with knowledge and insights that might not be obtained elsewhere.

XII

CANTATRIX IN LINGUAE UMBRARUM CANTAT

The student of the Wandering School should devote some time to the learning of modern languages. Any language other than our own native tongue, when studied, opens up new pathways of understanding within the mind and increases our efficacy as magicians. And any language tied to a specific tradition offers hidden insights into that tradition.

Learning a language is not as difficult as many believe. It is a question of attitude. If your attitude is that learning a language is an uphill struggle, then it will be an uphill struggle. If, on the other hand, your attitude is more relaxed and casual, then the struggle becomes a pleasant pastime – a simple game of brain teasers. Less effort leads to more progress, so long as the effort is made with regularity.

As they traverse foreign lands on their journey, students should immerse themselves in the language and culture of those lands and avoid the company of their compatriots.

MAGICAL LANGUAGE

The use of a 'magical language' of some sort, be it an actual language such as Latin or simply speaking in

XII. CANTATRIX IN LINGUAE UMBRARUM CANTAT

rhyme, is a basic technique for adding potency to any magical operation. Like putting on a special robe, it is in itself a declaration of magical intent.

Magical languages are a long-established feature of magic. The use of dead languages in Christian liturgy, such as Latin, Old Slavonic, and Coptic, and of biblical Hebrew in Jewish liturgy, is something we first see in Mesopotamia, where Sumerian was used as a liturgical language long after it had ceased to be a living one. As the ritual specialists who composed or recorded magical rites in antiquity and in medieval Europe were often themselves priests or rabbis, it is no surprise that liturgical languages such as Latin and Hebrew are a prominent feature of magical texts, but there are good reasons for the modern student to use them in incantations today. Firstly, they have become 'sacred' languages and as such have a numinous quality that facilitates the creation of a liminal space and a bridge to the spirit realms. Furthermore, they are a link to all those ancestors who would have heard these languages used in their churches or synagogues, and beyond them to those ancestors for whom they were living languages.

Additionally they can be used subversively in a number of ways, For example, when a witch uses the language of a priest, she is claiming equal status and power to a priest, thereby mocking the hubris of the priesthood. Another subversive factor has to do with the fact that these dead languages are effectively 'secret' languages, a category which also includes the use of barbarous names.

Barbarous names are another long-attested feature of magical incantations. It is often assumed that these names or words are described as being 'barbarous' because they are in some way 'barbaric' in the modern sense; however, they are so called because they are 'barbaric' in the original Greek sense of the word, namely that they are 'foreign sounding'.

In Ancient Greece, when Asians were thought to be powerful sorcerers, Asian-sounding incantations were employed in nocturnal rites to scare away unwanted visitors in times when native professional sorcerers were often executed for their impiety in attempting to bend the will of the gods.

This use of foreign-sounding words becomes, for the most part, a recitation of mysterious 'names' in the grimoires, although in the Venetian grimoire, the *Secrets of Solomon*, we still find foreign-sounding verses used in incantations, which include words taken from at least one actual foreign language, namely English. Modern languages, too, can be secret ones.

We see a modern language being used as a secret magical language portrayed in fiction in the 2017 TV series *Taboo* when the protagonist James Keziah Delaney (Tom Hardy) chants in Twi, and on various occasions does so in front of others, none of whom speak or understand Twi nor any other member of the Niger-Congo family of languages. In the series' nineteenth century London setting and indeed anywhere in Europe both then and now, Twi is a secret language.

Despite being unintelligible to the audience, they are aware that some form of rite is being performed,

XII. CANTATRIX IN LINGUAE UMBRARUM CANTAT

and in response their own imaginations lend potency to the spell being cast in a way that would not be possible were the language one they understood. It is a form of transgression and a demonstration of the meaning behind the word warlock in that it is a magical challenge to custom and tradition – in this instance the custom and tradition of nineteenth century Londoners.

In reality, however, this act would very likely result in laughter and derision, which would halt any incantation in its tracks and kill the spell. A far more practical use of modern languages as secret languages is simply to ensure that anyone who overhears it does not understand its content.

Welsh-speakers, for example, have a secret language. Welsh is often misrepresented by outsiders and London-centrics as being spoken by hardly anyone at all inside Wales, but in reality it is widely-spoken in Wales and is the majority language in the western half of the country, from Amlwch in the north to Llanelli in the south. Nevertheless, outside of 'Celtia' (the British Isles & Brittany), Welsh is about as obscure as a language can get. Most Europeans – indeed most people in the world outside of the Anglosphere – are completely unaware that Welsh exists. Thus Welsh, outside of Wales, is a secret language, and only one of many minority languages in Europe that are similarly obscure outside of their heartlands, such as Scottish Gaelic, Breton, and Basque. For that matter, the same can be said of various official state languages such as Icelandic, Finnish, Estonian, Latvian, Lithuanian, Hungarian, and Maltese, depending on how cosmopolitan a location we find ourselves in.

Historically there are also the slangs of the criminal underworld, the world of crooks, prostitutes, vagabonds, gamblers, Bohemians, and other denizens of the fringes of society which has included sorcerers since antiquity, and secret languages such as Thieves' Cant in England and Rotwelsch in Germany and Austria, first attested to in the thirteenth century, although here we stray away from the subject of magical language. Returning to that subject, let us consider the Demonic Macaronic.

DEMONIC MACARONIC

A 'macaronic' language is essentially a mash-up of two or more languages, and the term 'demonic macaronic' refers to that popular trope in fiction involving persons possessed by demons who respond to an exorcist using a mash-up of dead and foreign languages. A relatively recent example of the use of such a demonic macaronic is the 'Verbis Diablo' in the TV series *Penny Dreadful*, which combines the use of a demonic macaronic with that other popular diabolic trope, the reversed word or phrase.

The language was created by David J Peterson, who also created, among others, the Dothraki and Valyrian languages featured in another TV series, *Game of Thrones*.

Answering a question on the website Goodreads, Peterson said that:

> Verbis Diablo is different from anything I've ever done. First, it's a posteriori, which means

XII. CANTATRIX IN LINGUAE UMBRARUM CANTAT

that all the words and grammar come from other — in this case, real world — sources. Specifically, the sources were Arabic, Akkadian, Middle Egyptian, Attic Greek, Latin, Farsi and Turkish. Second, VD was not intended to be a language proper. I looked at the language as an art piece. VD is supposed to be a language twisted in form; wrenched from Earth's languages. Many words that meant something in a given language are taken and reversed phonetically to produce the equivalent VD word. Sometimes the reversal came with a reversal in meaning, as with justa, from Latin, which becomes *atsüü*, 'vile'. Also pieces of words from many different languages will often be combined to produce portmanteaux which may have nothing to do with the original meanings of any of the parts.

In addition, though there are patterns in the language, sometimes the patterns are broken for no reason. A word which has meant the same thing every time one has heard it will suddenly have a new meaning in a new sentence for no discernible reason. Words will change orders to subvert previously attested patterns; words will be pronounced differently for no reason at all; the auxiliary, one of the few bits of predictability in the language, will move or drop out entirely.

All of this combines to produce something that doesn't sound an awful lot like a language, and I think that's true. It defies attempts to learn it, meaning that the only way to actually speak it is to be touched by the Devil. In effect, that was the point.[30]

The TV series *The Exorcist* also uses a demonic macaronic, although a far less complex one, where one sentence or clause of a sentence might be, for example, in Aramaic and the next in German.

A demonic macaronic qualifies as a magical language; but it also has a more specific use, namely sacrilege. Sacrilege refers here to the 'breaking of the truce' we noted previously when discussing 'The Warlock and the Mouse', a device for engaging the denizens of the Other World. Saying the Lord's Prayer backwards is another example of this technique. What it is not, however, is an efficient means of communication with spirits.

In creating a 'Verbis Diablo' of our own, the most resonant languages are long-dead ones, the more ancient the better. Bearing in mind that communication is not a demonic macaronic's purpose, we don't have to concern ourselves with correct use of ancient grammars or even with a fixed vocabulary.

Our suggestions for creating a Verbis Diablo are as follows:

---

30 David J Peterson, *Goodreads* (2015) <https://www.goodreads.com/questions/428867-first-congratulations-on-both-your> [accessed 29 June 2025].

XII. CANTATRIX IN LINGUAE UMBRARUM CANTAT

1. Write down in normal everyday speech what we want said.
2. Translate it word for word in the same order as we have written down, switching language with each word.
3. Decide for ourselves which words or sentences we want to reverse, and whether or not the reversal of a word also signifies the reversal of its meaning.

As an example we shall translate the phrase 'I am thy king' into a mix of Sumerian, Akkadian, and Latin.

In Sumerian the phrase would be *ngae lugalzu imen*, but following the English word-order it would become *ngae imen zu lugal* (or, if following a Welsh word-order, it would need to add the word *zae*, 'thou', and become *zu lugal zae imen ngae*).

Following the English word-order, we reverse the word for 'king' to give it the meaning 'subject': *ngae imen zu lagul*, 'I am thy subject'.

We switch the Sumerian *ngae* to the Akkadian *anaku* and the Sumerian *imen* to the Latin *sum*: *anaku sum zu lagul*.

Rhyme, Whispers, and Song

As mentioned at the beginning of this chapter, the use of rhyme also qualifies as magical language, and rhyme has been used in incantation since antiquity. The language being used may not be a secret one, but it can become a secret language if the verses are whispered. *Cantatrix in linguae umbrarum cantat*, 'the witch chants in the language of shadows'. Some Scandinavian sorcerers are said to recite their incantations behind clenched teeth in order to maintain a spell's secrecy and thereby its potency.

The contrary is the case in other traditions: in the Welsh bardic tradition, a poem's potency lies in the skilful complexity of its composition; and in most traditions of song, the potency of a song lies in the vocal abilities of the singer or singers, and it is a potency more tangible to listeners than is usually the case with a chant or a whisper. Ultimately these different techniques will suit different occasions and circumstances.

XIII

VINDICTA VENEFICIO VINCIT

The Wiccan-inspired reluctance among modern practitioners of magic who self-identify as 'witches' to use magic with the intent of harming others is utterly alien to genuine witchcraft. Like all forms of practical magic, witchcraft exists as a means to acquire the things its practitioners require or desire, and historically in the case of practices labelled as 'witchcraft' the desire to cause harm and extract vengeance is almost always near the top of the list. It isn't called the Dark Art for nothing.

Most witches, warlocks, and cunning men of yore regularly slaughtered animals for sustenance, as was the norm in rural life; so it should come as no surprise that individuals capable of killing guiltless animals they had invested time, energy, and resources in tending to and caring for would lose not a wink of sleep in employing the Dark Art to punish those who had done them ill. A witch unwilling to consider casting such spells is little more than a hippy with a broomstick.

The Wiccan Threefold Law which states 'Ever mind the Rule of Three, three times your acts return to thee,' is dogmatic fluff and nonsense; nevertheless there are risks involved, should a curse be placed on someone merely for kicks or out of spite or pettiness. If the target is warded, the curse will most likely fail; worse still, if the target is a magician of any description, the person intending harm may find themselves hoisted with their own petard. Additionally, sedentary sorcerers who work at home or in a single workspace would be well-advised to find a separate and isolated location when engaging with the negative energies involved in curses.

Retribution is what a curse should be about, a justified desire for vengeance driven by righteous wrath or profound indignation – the qualities a curse requires for any reliable efficacy. Curses fuelled by these qualities are essentially about administering justice, and neither quality can be faked on a whim nor approximated by the sulks and hissy fits of narcissists. Without these qualities a curse runs the risk of being rendered ineffective by something as simple as a derisive smile. *Vindicta veneficio vincit*, 'with witchcraft, vengeance conquers'.

It is perhaps unsurprising that those who criticise the use of curses on the grounds that magic should only be used as part of a mystical pursuit of spiritual growth are almost invariably white middle-class men with little or no experience of chronic injustice.

We live in a world in which women have been raped, beaten, and killed by men every single day since the dawn of history, and this continues to be the case, even in socially progressive nations. In such circumstances as these the Wandering School recommends students become familiar with the casting of curses, especially female students, and encourages female students to travel together and in the long run to consider forming or joining a coven in order to pool their resources.

XIII. VINDICTA VENEFICIO VINCIT

Alumni of the Wandering School who go on to become service magicians will be approached by clients seeking assistance in addressing an injustice, which will more often than not require the use of curses.

When learning to curse, students should also learn to protect themselves from curses. It is easy to become paranoid about protection; students should trust in their allies to warn them when a curse has been cast against them, and otherwise generally trust in their amulets and allies to keep them safe, remembering to give regular offerings to their spirit allies in exchange for their protection.

Students can begin to familiarise themselves with the casting of curses with *The Little Book of Wicked Spells, Bindings and Retribution Magick* by M. Belanger, and how to protect themselves with *Deliverance: Hoodoo Spells of Uncrossing, Healing and Protection* by Khi Armand.

Exorcism by Knife

We shall end this prospectus with an excerpt from *British Goblins: Welsh Folklore, Fairy Mythology, Legends and Traditions* by Wirt Sikes:

> The exorcism by knife appears to be a Welsh notion; though there is an old superstition of wide prevalence in Europe that to give to or receive from a friend a knife or a pair of scissors cuts friendship. I have even encountered this superstition in America; once an editorial friend at Indianapolis gave

me a very handsome pocket-knife, which he refused to part with except at the price of one cent, lawful coin of the realm, asserting that we should become enemies without this precaution. In China, too, special charms are associated with knives, and a knife which has slain a fellow-being is an invaluable possession. In Wales, according to Jones, the Gwyllion often came into the houses of the people at Aberystruth, especially in stormy weather, and the inmates made them welcome – not through any love they bore them, but through fear of the hurts the Gwyllion might inflict if offended – by providing clean water for them, and taking especial care that no knife, or other cutting tool, should be in the corner near the fire, where the fairies would go to sit. 'For want of which care many were hurt by them.' While it was desirable to exorcise them when in the open air, it was not deemed prudent to display an inhospitable spirit towards any member of the fairy world. The cases of successful exorcism by knife are many, and nothing in the realm of faerie is better authenticated. There was Evan Thomas, who, travelling by night over Bedwellty Mountain, towards the valley of Ebwy Fawr, where his house and estate were, saw the Gwyllion on each side of him, some of them dancing around him in fantastic fashion. He also heard the sound of a bugle-horn winding in the air, and there seemed to be invisible hunters riding by. He then began to be afraid, but recollected his having heard that any person seeing Gwyllion may drive them away by drawing out a knife. So he drew out his knife, and the fairies vanished directly. Should we find, in tracing these notions back to their source that they are connected with Arthur's sword Excalibur? If so, there again we touch the primeval world.[31]

---

31 Wirt Sikes, *British Goblins: Welsh Folklore, Fairy Mythology, Legends and Traditions* (Sandycroft Publishing, 2017), pp. 42-43.

BIBLIOGRAPHY

Abusch, I. Tzvi, *Babylonian Witchcraft Literature* (Brown Judaic Studies, 1987)

Adams, Peter Mark, *The Game of Saturn* (Scarlet Imprint, 2018)

Andrews, Munya, *Journey into Dreamtime* (Ultimate World Publishing, 2020)

Andrews, Munya, *The Seven Sisters of the Pleiades: Stories from Around the World* (Spinifex Press, 2005)

Betz, Hans Dieter, *The Greek Magical Papyri in Translation* (University of Chicago Press, 1986)

Bobrowski, Jakub, *Mitologia słowiańska* (Bosz, 2017)

Carbonell Roura, Eudald & Tristan, Rosa Maria, *Atapuerca: 40 años inmersos en el pasado* (National Geographic, 2017)

Chart, David, *An Introduction to Shinto* (Mimusubi, 2020)

Contenau, Georges, *Everyday Life in Babylon and Assyria* (Edward Arnold, 1959)

Cross, Samuel Hazzard, *The Russian Primary Chronicle* (Medieval Academy of America, 2012)

Dalley, Stephanie, *Myths from Mesopotamia: Creation, The Flood, Gilgamesh and Others* (Oxford University Press revised edition, 2009)

Davies, W.W., *The Codes of Hammurabi and Moses* (Cornell University Library 2009)

Dickey, Matthew W, *Magic and Magicians in the Greco-Roman World* (Routledge, 2003)

Edmunds, Radcliffe G, *Drawing Down the Moon: Magic in the Ancient Greco-Roman World* (Princeton University Press, 2019)

Frankfurter, David, *Religion in Roman Egypt: Assimilaton and Resistance* (Princeton University Press, 1998)

BIBLIOGRAPHY

Halloran, John A., *Sumerian Lexicon* (Logogram Publishing, 2006)

Girtler, Roland, *Rotwelsch: Die alte Sprache der Gauner, Dirnen und Vagabunden* (Böhlau, Vienna, 2019)

Helle, Sophus, *Enheduana: The Complete Poems of the World's First Author* (Yale University Press, 2023)

Henken, Elissa, *National Redeemer: Owain Glyndŵr in the Welsh Tradition* (University of Wales Press, 1996)

Horning, Erik, *The Ancient Egyptian Books of the Afterlife* (Cornell University Press, 1999)

Hornblower, Simon, *The Oxford Classical Dictionary* (Oxford University Press, 2012)

Ifans, Dafydd & Rhiannon, *Y Mabinogion* (Gwasg Gomer, 2001)

Illes, Judika, *The Element Encyclopedia of 5000 Spells* (HarperElement, 2004)

Jacobsen, Thorkild, *Treasure of Darkness: A History of Mesopotamian Religion* (Yale University Press, 1976)

Jung, Carl Gustav, *Synchronicity: An Acausal Connecting Principle* (Princeton University Press, 1960)

Kadmus, *True to the Earth* (Gods & Radicals Press, 2018)

Klutstein, Ilana, *Marsilio Ficino et la theologie ancienne* (L.S. Olschki, 1987)

Lewis, Charlton & Short, Charles, *A Latin Dictionary* (Nigel Gourlay, 2020)

Machen, Arthur, *The Memoirs of Jacques Casanova de Seingalt* (New York, Putnam, 1902

Morus-Baird, Gwilym, *Taliesin Origins: Exploring the Myth of the greatest Celtic Bard* (Celtic Source, 2023)

Nelson, John K., *A Year in the Life of a Shinto Shrine* (University of Washington Press, 1996)

Ovid, *Fasti* (Harvard University Press, 1931)

Ovid, *Metamorphoses* (Penguin Classics, 2014)

Peterson, David J, *Goodreads* (2015) <https://www.goodreads.com/questions/428867-first-congratulations-on-both-your> [accessed 29 June 2025]

Peterson, Joseph H., *The Secrets of Solomon* (Twilight Grotto, 2018)
Porterfield, Professor Charles, *The Sporting Life* (Lucky Mojo Curio Company, 2016)
Rankine, David, *The Grimoire Encyclopaedia* Volume 1 (Hadean Press, 2023)
Reas, Jason, *Fox Magic: Handbook of Chinese Witchcraft and Alchemy in the Fox Tradition* (Mandrake, 2021)
Ritner, Robert Kriech, *The Mechanics of Ancient Egyptian Magical Practice* (Oriental Institute, Chicago, 1993)
Robinson, Mairi, *The Concise Scots Dictionary* (Mercat Press, 1992)
Seddon, Christopher, *Prehistoric Investigations* (Glanville, 2016)
Simón, Francisco Marco, *Cultus Deorum: La religión en la antigua Roma* (Sintesis, 2021)
Sikes, Wirt, *British Goblins: Welsh Folklore, Fairy Mythology, Legends and Traditions* (Public Domain)
Spence, Lewis, *Myths and Legends of Ancient Egypt* (George C Harrap & Co London, 1915)
Stratton-Kent, Jake, *Geosophia: The Argo of Magic* Vols I & II (Scarlet Imprint, 2010)
Sykes, Rebecca Wragg, *Kindred: Neanderthal Life, Love, Death and Art* (Bloomsbury, 2020)
Tannen, Ricki Stefanie, *The Female Trickster: The Mask that Reveals* (Routledge, 2007)
Taylor, Thomas, *Hymns and Initiations* (Prometheus Trust, 1995)
Thomas, Gwyn, *Gair am Air* (University of Wales Press, 2000)
Various authors, *When Neanderthals and Modern Humans Met* (Kerns Verlag, 2006)
Vaudoise, Mallorie, *Honoring Your Ancestors: A Guide to Ancestral Veneration* (Llewellyn, 2019)
Wales, University of, *Geiriadur Prifysgol Cymru* (University of Wales Press, 1967 – 2002)
Warnock, Christopher, *Secrets of Planetary Ritual* (Lulu,

2020)
Young, Paul Summers, *Enchiridion Leonis Papae* (Black Letter Press, 2022)
Zelazny, Roger, *A Night in the Lonesome October* (William Morrow & Co., 1993)

Recommended Books

Armand, Khi, *Deliverance: Hoodoo Spells of Uncrossing, Healing and Protection* (Missionary Independent Spiritual Church, 2015),
Belanger M., *The Little Book of Wicked Spells, Bindings and Retribution Magick* (Hadean Press, 2022)
Dalley, Stephanie, *Myths from Mesopotamia: Creation, The Flood, Gilgamesh and Others* (Oxford University Press, 2009)
George, Demetra, *Ancient Astrology in Theory and Practice* Volume 1 (Rubedo Press, 2019)
George, Demetra, *Ancient Astrology in Theory and Practice* Volume 2 (Rubedo Press, 2022)
Greer, John Michael & Warnock, Christopher, *The Complete Picatrix* (Lulu, 2011)
Hansen, John, *Communing with the Spirits: The Magical Practice of Necromancy* (Xlibris, 2005)
Harms, Daniel, *The Long-Lost Friend* (Llewellyn, 2012)
Helle, Sophus, *Enheduana* (Yale University Press, 2023)
Horning, Erik, *The Ancient Egyptian Books of the Afterlife* (Cornell University Press, 1999)
Huson, Paul, *Mastering Herbalism* (Madison Books, 2001)
Huson, Paul, *Mastering Witchcraft* (iUniverse, 2006)
Jacobsen, Thorkild, *Treasure of Darkness* (Yale University Press, 1976)
Karr, Don & Skinner, Stephen, *The Book of the Moon – Liber Lunae* (Llewellyn, 2018)
Lilly, William. *Christian Astrology Books 1 & 2* (Astrology

Center of America, 2005)
Lilly, William, *Christian Astrology Book 3* (Astrology Center of America, 2005)
Marie, Mama, *The Hoodoo Bible* (Independent, 2021)
Miller, Jason, *Consorting with Spirits* (Red Wheel Weiser, 2022)
Peterson, Joseph, *The Clavis or Key of the Magic of Solomon* (Ibis, 2009)
Peterson, Joseph, *True Black Magic* (CreateSpace, 2917)
Peterson, Joseph, *Elucidation of Necromancy* (Ibis, 2021)
Peterson, Joseph, *The Sixth and Seventh Book of Moses* (Hays, 2008)
Porterfield, Professor Charles, *A Deck of Spells* (Lucky Mojo Curio Company, 2015)
Porterfield, Professor Charles, *The Sporting Life* (Lucky Mojo Curio Company, 2016)
Rankine, David, *The Grimoire Encyclopaedia* Volume 1 (Hadean Press, 2023)
Rankine, David, *Claves Intelligentiarum* (Hadean Press, 2024)
Rankine, David, *The Grimoire of Arthur Gauntlet* (Avalonia, 2011)
Rankine, David, *The Book of Gold* (Avalonia, 2010)
Skinner, Stephen & Rankine, David, *The Veritable Key of Solomon* (Llewellyn, 2008)
Spence, Lewis, *Myths and Legends of Ancient Egypt* (Forgotten Books, 2017)
Stratton-Kent, Jake, Night School Volume 1: *The Sworn and Secret Grimoire* (Hadean Press, 2021)
Stratton-Kent, Jake, Night School Volume 2: *Cyprian's Offices of Spirits* (Hadean Press,, 2024)
Wachter, Aidan, *Six Ways* (Ygret Niche Publishing, 2018)
Warnock, Christopher, *Secrets of Planetary Ritual* (Lulu, 2009)
Warnock, Christopher, *Mansions of the Moon* (Lulu, 2010)

Young, Paul Summers, *Enchiridion Leonis Papae* (Black Letter Press, 2022)

Yronwode, Catherine, *Hoodoo Herb and Root Magic* (Lucky Mojo Curio Company, 2002)

INDEX

A

Amaterasu 29
ancestors
  and magical language 93
  and mythology 76
  as local spirits 71
  divine 29
  establishing relationships with 35, 37, 38-39
  in the Netherworld 42
animism 27, 32-33
ašipu 18
astrology 47-48 *See also* Seven Planets.
  and the planets 49

B

barbarous names 93
bibliomancy 73, 78
book of shadows 9

C

Casanova, Giacomo 2, 12
Code of Hammurabi 1, 17
Count of St Germain 2
Crowley, Aleister 2

D

Dayworld 40
Devil (the) 23, 83-84, 87 *See also* Pan, Veles.
divination 72, 73-74

bibliomancy 81
dreaming 32-33

F

fairies 27, 29, 104-105
feria 89, 90
folk magic 9-12, 78
forum 88, 90

G

ghosts 18, 31
Goetia 47
Greek Magical Papyri 19, 22
grimoire 9, 11-12, 78

H

Hebrew Bible 77-78heroes 30, 42
heteropraxy 20
Holy Rosary 37, 69
planetary hymns *See also* Seven Planets.
  Hymn to Jupiter 59
  Hymn to Mars 54-55
  Hymn to Mercury 57
  Hymn to Saturn 65
  Hymn to The Moon 52
  Hymn to the Sun 67
  Hymn to Venus 62

I

illicit magic 1, 17-18
imagination 7-8
itinerant magicians 2, 16, 33, 48, 50, 71, 88

K

kami 27-33

L

licit magic 1, 17, 18
Luna 50, 51, 52, 68, 69

M

magical language 92-95 *See also* secret language.
  demonic macaronic 96-98
magical orders 3
Manawydan 24–25
mythology 26, 72-73
  ancient 79-80
  and cosmology 42-43
  classical 78
  medieval 78-79
  myth cycles 29
  narratives 75-77

N

Netherworld 40-44

O

Occult Revival 5
offerings 20, 30-31, 33, 37, 39, 52, 103
Orphic Hymn to Pan 86
orthopraxy 20
Otherworld 2, 24

P

Pan 83, 85-87, 88
pastura 90-91
Pax Deorum 28
Planetary hours 68
Pliny 80
psalms 35

R

rationalism 5, 8
red 40, 41, 42
retribution magic 102-103
Rhonabwy 45-46

S

secrecy 15-16
secret language 93-96
seven
  planets 50-68
  spirits 47-48, 69
Shinto 20, 27-28, 31, 33
spirits 6-7, 8, 15, 20, 27, 31, 32-34 *See also* kami, seven spirits.
  allies 10, 19, 26, 90, 103
  ancestral *See* ancestors.
  communication 73-74, 98
  encountering in dreams 44-45, 46
  local 71-72
  malevolent 18
  nature 29, 30
Stratton-Kent, Jake 2, 47
synchronicities 2, 71-73, 76

T

theatre of operations 88
The Road 2
truce 23, 24, 98

V

Veles 83, 84-85, 87, 88
  as trickster 84, 87

W

warlock 17-18, 23, 95
Western Tradition 1, 48, 79
witchcraft 17-18, 32, 101-102

Y

yokai 31

www.ingramcontent.com/pod-product-compliance
Lightning Source LLC
Chambersburg PA
CBHW060837170426
43192CB00019BA/2808